Contents

ACKNOWLEDGMENTS AND THANKS

This book was thought to have served its purpose in the ten years of its life. Supporters of the "Wellclose" rescue work have, however thought otherwise and, with the generous help of a voluntary worker, a new edition now appears under the Mowbray imprint.

I am most grateful to Bishop Trevor of Stepney for writing the preface. His personal interest in the work goes back to my early days when he visited Father Neville at 84 Cable Street.

Two photographers have covered the rescue work and given their services. Frank Rust has followed me with his camera for twenty years, and was one of my churchwardens at St Paul's Dock Street. With the same devotion Harry Wills has covered the Birmingham work for Angela Butler, and has helped in countless ways.

The painter of the portrait on the front cover, Carl Geri, came to me out of the blue with his friendship and his art. He has given the portrait to me and hopes it may be of use to the fund and I thank him.

I am in debt to so many who cannot be mentioned individually, but I must take this special chance to thank my wife for her constant sharing of the work we are all engaged in.

Preface

I feel it to be almost an impertinence to write a preface for this new edition of *Father Joe*. After all, I have been in Stepney for a short five years and I am only just beginning to feel confident that I know what I am talking about. Joseph Williamson, a born East Ender, can speak with absolute authority, and has done so in this book. But there are three reasons which have decided me to do what I am asked. First, because it is the author himself who requested the preface—and who has ever been able to resist Father Joe? The pages of this book tell of those who have tried, and of the futility of such an exercise! Secondly, because the work of the house in Wellclose Square continues to be of tremendous importance to the life of the whole Stepney community, and of equally tremendous significance to the Church in East London. It would be, quite literally, a tragedy if such work were allowed to be forgotten or overlooked because of false assumptions about the state of our society today. Yet it cannot be properly understood or assessed without some knowledge of its origins. And its origins are all disclosed by Father Joe in the description of his own great life and ministry.

But there is yet another reason for a fresh preface (though not, I'm glad to say, a substitute for the original foreword by Archbishop George Appleton) and that is the fantastic change that has taken place in Cable Street since this book was published ten years ago.

It is true that Wellclose Square is recognisably the same place that it was: especially the house and school buildings which dominate it. But the rest of the street has been almost entirely redeveloped: the old squalor replaced by new tidiness, the old slums by new flats and maisonettes. Building is still continuing (over 260 new homes are going up opposite St Mary's Church), and there is only a block or two of the street as it used to be; but demolition is almost complete.

Over the whole area looms the greatest redevelopment scheme that London has experienced in a century: the rebuilding and the renewal of London's Docklands. Within the next twenty years or less East London will have been physically transformed.

It is *because* of change, and because of the pace of change that the social problems of East London remain acute. Tower Hamlets (the borough which now comprises the old East End boroughs of which Stepney was one) has an unenviable record—or rather, several records. The illegitimacy rate: the truancy rate and the juvenile delinquency rate are all significantly higher than in any other London borough. The number of children officially "in care" is appallingly large: one child in twenty-nine—or one child in every classroom in every school. The number of schizophrenics is twice as high, we are told by the Psychiatric Rehabilitation Association, as in any other place. Yet now—as when this book was written—most of these statistics reflect social evils which have not *originated* from within the local community at all. The girls who find their way to Wellclose Square—and the house is generally full—are nearly always strangers to the East End or to London itself.

We live in an affluent society and a mobile society. Stepney today is as deeply affected by these two trends as anyone else. Its deprivation is no longer the kind that Father Joe describes when writing of his own childhood. But it is a deep and cruel deprivation none the less. It is what Mother Teresa of Calcutta so movingly describes as a deprivation of love.

Father Joe and the work he founded and still so vigorously champions represent the answer to that deprivation.

The motto for this book might well be the words of the great 16th century mystic St John of the Cross:

"In the evening of life, we shall be judged by love"

✠ Trevor Huddleston CR
Bishop of Stepney
1 May 1973

Foreword

by Archbishop George Appleton

> My candle burns at both ends;
> It will not last the night;
> But oh, my foes, and oh, my friends—
> It gives a lovely light.

THAT is what Father Joe has been doing for the past ten years—burning all his candles at both ends. The result has been a light which has been recognised not only in Stepney, but, thanks to the reporters and photographers of the Press, recognising not only news but sincerity and fire, throughout the whole country and indeed beyond.

Such extravagance burns up the man, so it is no wonder that Father Joe has felt compelled to resign his living in order to devote his remaining strength and time to the fight against vice, the rescue of its victims and the strengthening of the work he has founded.

It is therefore a matter of great thankfulness that under the pressure of friends he has found time to write down the story of his experiences in East London, at the two ends of his life.

I first met Joseph Williamson forty-two years ago when we were both freshmen at the theological and missionary college of St. Augustine, Canterbury. I think that what drew us together in the first place was the fact that we both came from poor homes. I came from a country grammar school to which I had been fortunate enough to gain a scholarship. He came from army service in the First World War, via the training school at Knuts-

9

ford, which provided men with the preparatory education necessary to enable them to study for ordination. He was able to teach
me a good deal about life; I was able to help him in his studies.
We have kept in touch ever since, and finally found ourselves in
neighbouring parishes in East London, both facing considerable
social problems.

Father Joe has given me the manuscript of his story to read.
I read it through at one sitting, so moving and fascinating did I
find it. His story of East London sixty years ago, with its poverty
and heartbreak, gives a picture of social conditions which must
make all who knew them and who can enter into them through
his vivid memory, thank God for the Welfare State, even if it does
have its many casualties.

"Son of my mother, I was made in her image." This book is a
tribute to Lucy Williamson; no greater or shorter tribute could be
paid to her than the words of her son, just quoted. I well remember the pride and love in her face as she waited on the steps of
St. Paul's Cathedral for her son who had just been ordained by
Bishop Winnington-Ingram. She never ceased to wonder that she,
who could neither read nor write, had a son who was now a priest
of the Church. Her years of scrubbing the dirty greasy smocks of
butchers, the countless meals she had gone without, had brought
this almost unbelievable blessing.

Joe was never ashamed of his family or of East London. All
through his life the child was father of the man-to-be. His anger
against the awful housing conditions of 1962 goes back to his own
experience of the 1890's. His burning desire to do something to
help prostitutes today goes back to the horror of a visit to a Red
Lamp brothel behind the lines in France during the First World
War.

An autobiography can be very revealing, often in ways of which
the writer is not conscious. Father Joe has never been one to think
of the impression he is arousing in the minds of the spectators.
Wherever he has sensed injustice he has been quick to speak,
wherever anyone was in need of defence or rescue he has not
hesitated to dash in. He has always been ready to rescue any
maiden in distress, and if the knightly journey took him by Lam-

beth Palace, Fulham Palace or 10 Downing Street, he would pause to summon the eminent residents to join in the crusade, or on occasion send a rocket missive to all the episcopal residences of the Church of England or an earnest appeal to Buckingham Palace.

If anyone went to visit him, as I often did, the visitor would be welcomed in, offered his choice of every kind of hospitality, and then treated to a flood of vivid eloquence, not always too coherent, but in which the man and his fire made the impression rather than his words, and in which the solitary listener obviously became a public meeting, needing to be convinced and converted. His favourite adjective is "ruddy", a combination of the frustration attached to the more popular rhyming word with a kind of humorous recognition that there were certain difficulties in the situation under review. Or sometimes an indication of complete agreement, as when I occasionally got in a word or two, as he paused for breath, and was commended with the words, "Chum, you're ruddy well right."

Joe was always an independent worker, impatient, finding it difficult to wait until the next committee meeting to get a new course of action launched. Indeed, it was with great difficulty that he was persuaded to have a committee at all. It was at this point that I became intimately associated with his work, for he was willing to try a committee if I would be its chairman. He knew that from time to time I should disagree with him, but he trusted me to understand what was in his mind. Once the committee was in being, he realised that its members were all out to forward his plans, and became remarkably disciplined in his interventions and in his readiness to let us find some alternative way of achieving some particular purpose. Occasionally the chairman had to suggest quietly and firmly that the committee's job was not to right every wrong or accept responsibility for every situation, but to tackle prostitution and the factors involved in it.

It soon became clear that bad housing was one of the chief factors in the Cable Street situation and this led to a tremendous and magnificent campaign, in which he was greatly helped by Frank Rust, his press photographer churchwarden, and by

Edith Ramsay, a veteran social worker in East London. Never was a parish magazine used for such dynamic purpose as the "Pilot", hardly ever can there have been such uninhibited hard hitting, without respect of person, rank or party.

A man of such divine impatience is inevitably hard on his friends. I doubt if he ever fully realised the vital part that his wife Audrey played in it all—always ready to provide hospitality, always ready to drive one of the girls to hospital, always cheerful and quick to do what was necessary to ease the restless impatience and sudden impulses of her dynamo of a husband, while all the time longing for the quiet of the countryside and her flower garden, or feeling the draw of her growing number of grand-children.

Joe has paid generous tribute to Nora Neal, who is mother to the girls who come to Wellclose Square, ready at any time of day or night to give them a warm and disarming welcome. Daphne Jones makes a different contribution: she is at home in the cafés and brothels, speaks the language as it were, and incidentally is a trained midwife, whose services are bound to be needed sooner or later. These two are regarded with great affection by the girls who have been in and out of Church House; a year or two back when the House had to be closed temporarily to give the two workers their much-needed annual holiday, a deputation of girls from the neighbourhood came to protest, asking, "What are we to do while you two are away?"

It is the west end of Cable Street which is the centre of the worst vice; it must not be assumed that the whole of Stepney is as bad. Indeed those who live in other parts of the borough are critical that the name of Stepney should be so often associated with the trade in women's bodies. In the early stages of Church House a careful record was kept of the girls who came for a period, and it was found that out of ninety different girls only one was a Londoner. The rest came from industrial towns in the north and from Scotland and Ireland. Another interesting fact was that almost all the girls came from broken homes. It seemed as if they were searching in some mysterious way of their own for a love which they had never received.

Why then do these girls come to Cable Street? Mainly because the demand is there. East London has always been a place to which people have come in search of work or to lose their identity for a time. The docks are there, and many men hope to pick up casual labour or to get a job in a ship. Nowadays, British Road Services has a big centre near by, in which lorry drivers park for the night before loading up. There are no proper hostels for them, and the cafés are open all night. Often girls from the north are given lifts in the lorries coming to the docks and gratitude on top of a few drinks or the need of a place for the night is the first step downwards, from which it is difficult to recover.

The situation is made more complicated by the number of people from overseas who have come to live in this part of London —West Indians, West Africans, Somalis, Pakistanis, Maltese and Cypriots. Most of them arrive without their womenfolk, at the start anyhow, and being deprived of the usual married life, many of them are ready to pay for substitutes, while others, particularly Maltese and Cypriots, are ready to exploit the situation by opening cafes and clubs, where British girls are on hire to the men of any nation.

However, Father Joe and Wellclose Square are now well known, and the word passes round that the escape hatch is via Wellclose Square. Let two women who have used this escape hatch tell their own story:

First Judy:

"It happened on a Sunday when I was feeling rather depressed and fed up with my way of life. I was all alone in my flat, and, picking up one of the Sunday newspapers, came across an article by the Rev. Joe Williamson about the terrible sordid vice that was going on in his parish of Stepney. I was very much impressed by this article, and by the good work that this noble priest was trying to do, more or less single-handed, against tremendous odds, with only a handful of faithful helpers to help him in his fight to save not only the souls, but to rescue unfortunate girls before they were dragged right down in the gutter—and indeed I now know that he has even done just that—he has even stretched his hand and his heart out, and taken girls out of the gutter.

"When I had finished reading the article I thought, here is a man who has got everything—everything that I needed, and wanted, and had long been searching for. Here was a man with an outstretched hand, with love in his heart for the mentally and physically worn, down-trodden social outcasts of my world—the prostitutes. For I myself was such a person, and although my beat and my life were on a more luxurious scale than the unfortunate girls of Stepney, basically it works out the same—soul-destroying, degrading, and a bloody awful way of life.

"Then and there I sat down and wrote a letter to the Rev. Williamson, to congratulate him on the work he was doing, and to urge him to continue the fight. I received in return an invitation to call at the vicarage and have tea, and so got my first introduction to Father Joe and his charming and practical wife. Looking back on that afternoon, which was to be a turning point in my life, my memories are of the warm welcome extended to me . . . I shall never forget them both. Always they will have a place in my heart, and I shall be eternally grateful to them. For they made me see the light, and change my ways from the sordid, seamy life of London Town, to become the away-from-it-all, happy girl I am now . . .

"I am a Roman Catholic, although while I was living in sin and walking the streets, not a practising one. Never once did Father Joe try to win me over to his own Church, but always he kept advising me to go and call on my own parish priest and seek his help . . . If only I had met such a man as Father Joe years ago, what heartbreak, what worry, sadness and tears, I would have avoided. I might have met a good Catholic man, been married in a church, and been the proud possessor of a home and children. On that score I shall always walk alone . . .

"I owe that good priest a hell of a lot. He has put me on the right road, and for me there just will be no going back. I have reached the point of no return. I did not always allow myself to put him on the high pedestal on which he now stands. I have knocked around far too much—and been knocked around by a lot of vile men—to put my trust in the first Holy Joe that came my way. At the start I took all his promises, and his pleadings, with a pinch of salt. After all, why should I trust him, or any other man? But this disbelief was very quickly dispelled on my knowing Father Joe. May the good Lord bless him, and his wife, and his faithful band of helpers."

And now Miriam:

"I first came in contact with Father Joe after being picked up by a policewoman just after being thrown out of a café, because I had fallen to sleep in there. I was completely exhausted, I hadn't had anywhere to stay for a few weeks or a square meal for a long time. The policewoman took me to Church House, where Miss Neal, Father Joe's assistant, took me in, gave me a bath and a meal and put me to bed. At the time, to me, this was nothing short of a miracle. To think that just a few hours ago I had been thinking of throwing myself off Tower Bridge and everything had looked so black, and there seemed no hope of ever getting away from the company of ponces, prostitutes, drug addicts and all the other criminals and riff-raff.

"I met Father Joe in person the next day, and I liked him from the start, he had a great effect on my thinking and helped me to see some of the things that were right and some of them that were wrong. I am not going to say that he turned me from bad to good just like that, for Father Joe and I have had many disagreements since we first met and even after I met him I slipped from bad to worse, disregarded all his advice and rejected all his help and ended as a drug addict. But even after I slipped to this level he never gave up trying to make me see how wrong this was and in the end I did begin to see what a fool I was being. And so I gave up living like I was and started trying to live a decent life which I am now doing and I am very happy, thanks to Father Joe and his assistants. I would like to say that if Father Joe had just been a normal preacher all the talking on earth would not have had the slightest influence on me. As it is, I shall never forget him and his two wonderful women helpers, Miss Neal and Miss Jones."

Father Joe's story is a tribute to the Church in East London. He himself is the product of generations of devoted Anglo-Catholic priests—Dolling, Wainwright, Dawson, Lambert, Wilson—who brought the love of God to the poorest and saddest homes, who brought colour and beauty and warmth to their churches, and gave their people a spiritual training, a memory which would recall them to penitence, forgiveness and duty however far and however often they might stray in later life. In Joseph Williamson, a new name has been added to the list of honour.

Father Joe is an example of what God can do given faith and courage, bringing to light and brilliance the true gem in a rough human diamond, willing to be cut and shaped by a Master hand.

PART ONE

POPLAR

CHAPTER I

My Family
and Early Childhood

MY mother went to work when she was nine years old in the year 1872. She was one of a big family living in Limehouse, East London. Her father was a kindly man, a coachman by trade, but her mother was hard, often brutal to her children, although she was sober and efficient. Lucy Rebecca Payne never went to school and could neither read nor write. She went into service when she was nine years old and was paid 2s. 6d. a week. Soon after beginning work she was given a sheet to wash and was told how well she had done it. As a reward she was given all the washing to do in addition to all the other household work, except the cooking. When she let fall a sheet she was hanging on the line, she had her knuckles rapped with a stick. She worked from early morning until late at night.

At the age of fifteen, without her parents' knowledge and giving her age as twenty, she married George Williamson, a sailor. She was married at St. Paul's, Burdett Road, generally known as "Cotton's Church"—Cotton was the name of the vicar. It was two years before she told her mother, and then only because her firstborn, Esther, was on the way. My grandmother was to the point: "You have made your bed; now you must lie in it," she said. She helped Mother to find a room and Esther was born in 1880. Mother never stopped working after she was married, except for a day or two after the babies arrived. She was never ill until she was in her sixties.

She was a very strong and healthy-looking woman, with a fine complexion. The power she had to go on, in seemingly hopeless conditions, came from an inner spiritual strength, and although she had strong determination there was an ease, an assurance about her which carried her. So far as one could gather it had nothing to do with religious practices. Yet it drew forth ejaculations like, "God help us," and moved her in times of want to complete trust, for she would say with the deepest feeling, "God has never left us without a loaf." As children we saw too the blackest depths of depression when she felt near to being beaten. "I can't go on," she would cry, and I remember how my sisters and I would hug her head crying, "Don't, Mother." Our home was like a dead house and her dreadful sobs shook us all. Displays of sadness and tears before us were very few, but they were terrible. She must have endured most of her fits of depression alone, probably in the streets, where I think she walked them off. She was always loving and kind. There was no cruelty in her, nor could she bear to see it. Once when she was near the end of her tether an exclamation of despair slipped out. We heard her cry, "I must go and drown myself." It meant she could see no escape from the everlasting grinding poverty and the agony of watching her little ones go hungry.

I recently got my friend Frank Rust to go with me to my Poplar area of Hill Place Street, Cothall Street, and Arcadia Street, to take some photographs. We went first to Limehouse Cut by the "River Head" and Cothall Street, where in the old days, sixty years ago, there was only a simple rail to keep people from the towing path of the canal. Adults had had no difficulty in putting a leg over the rail and reaching the ground on the other side. Children could just slip through. The railing might well not have been there at all for all the protection it gave. Having got through the railings, just two yards of earth separated us from the deep canal, a water way for barges which are even now drawn by horses, but in the old days were more often pushed along by hook and pole men. This traffic took goods from the docks to the factories lining the "Cut" and vice versa. That 200 yards of Cothall Street going from the "River Head" to the "Prince of Wales" on Stinkhouse Bridge gave us the horrors, though it is

amazing what you can get used to. Two or three times a week
there would be a cry and a rush—"Someone in the Cut." For the
most part the people who managed to drown themselves were
women. Usually it was at week-ends.

Week-ends! On Saturday at 1 o'clock the men were paid, if
they were in work, but most men seemed to be out of work so
there was nothing to eat for the family. Men, as well as the
children, turned to Mother, as if she were a magician, for food.
Most mothers got food, God knows how, but some of them could
stand it no longer, so to the "Cut" they went and ended it all. It
was a tragic occurrence.

If Mother had died when we were young, we would have been
taken to Langley House, the East London Orphanage, still in
existence. I can see the herded orphans now, the little girls and
boys, in grey and red. The girls wore grey hats, grey capes and
long grey frocks. They looked like rows of pathetic little old
women, and even though they had a good bed and a belly full of
food, and we had little or none, we felt sorry for them. I still do,
for nothing on this earth can make up for a natural mother's love
and care.

My father died tragically on 30th January 1897, the day before
my mother's birthday—she was just thirty-five. An old photograph showed him as a very good-looking man with dark hair
and a full moustache. He was a very strong man. He was working
for a ship-breaking firm by the name of Cohen. An old ship's
boiler was being broken up with chisel and hammer in the East
India Docks, the "Mud Dock" as that part was then called. The
boiler fell apart and hit my father, crushing him into the mud.
He was taken to Poplar Hospital, where he died. When my mother
saw him, his hair had turned completely white. I can just remember being lifted up to see him in his coffin—I was only three at
the time. I felt nothing but a sense of amusement and made some
remark about his "whiskers". Not until many years later was I to
realise what that meant to my mother.

The harshness of the times allowed no responsibility for
accident or death to fall on the employer. Mother had to bury my
father in the cheapest way and bear the expense. It was a terrible

disgrace in those days for anyone to be buried by the "parish" and to have a pauper's funeral. So people borrowed what the insurance did not cover, and neighbours had a whip-round and gave their coppers for a friend.

Mother had eleven children in all. She lost three in infancy so she had eight when Father died, the youngest but a few months old. She was left with fourpence in the world, and George, my eldest brother, was bringing in a few shillings as a lad of fourteen. She went to the Poplar Board of Guardians, where Mr. Will Crooks, one of the earliest Labour Members of Parliament, was chairman. Temporarily he granted Mother some loaves of bread and five shillings a week, and when she reported again in a fortnight's time, he offered to take the four youngest of us into Langley House—"That will help you to work for the others and get straight."

Mother refused to let us go. Will Crooks was furious, and pointed to himself as an example of what an orphanage could turn out. Finally he asked, "What would they not have that they have got now?" When Mother replied, "A mother's love," they laughed at her. She was told that she would get no help, and that "if it were found that she was neglecting the children, they would make it as hot as they could for her." Mother thanked them and left.

The fact was that when men could not find work they were hopeless and helpless, whereas mothers would walk the streets, clean doorsteps and windows, plead, beg, and even sell themselves for bread for their little ones and their husbands. Nobody knew how they got it, nobody asked; the bread was there and Mother was wonderful for getting it.

When my mother was in funds—sixpence did wonders in those days—she would buy "three penn'orth of pieces" (bits of meat), and "a penn'orth of pot'erbs" (carrots, turnips and onions), add potatoes and dumplings, and make a wonderful stew. There was always some over to send to Dick Sykes who lived opposite. Dick's legs were crippled and doubled up under him, and the only way he could get about was to rest the lower part of his chest on the axle of two iron wheels and propel himself along by the backs of his hands. His mother neglected him, going out to work all day and leaving him no food.

How my mother existed is a mystery. I am reminded of the Lord's saying: "I have meat ye know not of." She would sit at table watching us eat, and she would make little balls of dry bread and put them in her mouth. One of us would urge her: "Have some dinner, Mother," and she would reply quite cheerfully: "I'll have mine presently." I cannot remember her having a proper meal with us when we were children. I am sure she lived on heavenly food in those days, for she had little or no earthly food. "God has never left us without a loaf," she would say, and somehow we got bread enough.

It was a strange life we lived. I slept in a tiny room in which there were two beds. I shared one with my brother Tom, and our elder brother Albert slept in a tiny bed alone. I can't remember where the rest slept.

Mother did a lot of work at home; heaps of washing and ironing. In winter we never saw the fire, for washing was always being dried by it. When other women went out to work, she would have their babies in and care for them; all for love, of course. She would talk to them, sing to them, wash them and love them just as she did us. On one occasion my brother Will came in to find the kitchen full of other people's children, two of them ill. "What can I do with the poor mites?" Mother said, when he complained. "Their mother must work." Will threatened to hang a board outside, saying "Home for little children at 18 Hill Place Street."

The fact is, Mother just could not resist helping people in trouble. She had a heart as big as the world, and she had no fear. We often worried what would happen to her when she intervened for the weak and stopped rows and fights, but she was always respected.

Our baker in Hill Place Street had a very young niece sent from Germany to help his wife—all our bread in Poplar was baked by Germans until the 1914 War. The baker was baking all night, his shop was opened about 6.30 a.m. and his wife did the serving. The little niece, not more than ten or eleven years old, was treated as a slave. The biggest of baker's baskets was used to carry a dozen or more loaves to the shops, and the little girl had to carry the basket. One bitterly cold morning my mother saw her struggling with her huge load and crying bitterly. She went straight to the baker's wife and told her what she thought of her. The woman was furious and picked up the bread knife, threatening to kill the little girl. But Mother caught her wrist, secured the knife, and then called up the baker and made him promise to send the child back home to Germany.

Later, when the 1914 War was declared, it was a signal to many East Londoners to smash up and loot all the German shops and houses. Our baker's wife was expecting a baby at that time, and she had not long to go. The shop windows were broken, and men were inside throwing the loaves out to the people, while the woman crouched in fear in a corner. Without hesitation, Mother went through the crowd, pulled two men out of the shop, placed herself in the doorway and appealed to the crowd on behalf of the woman. There she stayed until the police came and took the Germans away to safety.

Many a time I have known her to intervene in a fight between two brothers who lived a few houses down the road. They were big, tough men, who drank heavily, and their sister Lizzie, a refined and gracious girl not fitted for the rough and tumble of Poplar life, was unable to stop them. She would come crying to Mother, and Mother would go and tell the men just what she thought of them, and what they were doing to their poor sister. They would break down and allow themelves to be led quietly away from the scene of the fight.

I remember wondering why people allowed her to interfere in their lives and quarrels. The clue came in a letter I had from a friend, who wrote: "What a great lady she was; she had grace, she had taste, she hated unkindness, she was respected and loved by all who knew her. And Poplar knew her."

She had problems enough with her own family. My eldest brother George had a hard time, and it made him grim and tough. It was easy to get into trouble in those days, and the punishment was harsh. George and a friend pulled a neck handkerchief, valued at ninepence, from a bundle tied up for sale outside a shop. George got all the blame, and was sent to the Reformatory School at Redhill for five years. He had never been in any trouble before. He had been top of his class at Alton Street School. Mother was worried, but never dreamed that he would be so harshly treated. The other boy, who had in fact pulled the handkerchief down, got off. His mother had gone round to all the influential people she could on behalf of her boy. Poor Mother had felt she could not lose a day's work, and suffered agony when she realised what she might have done.

To get to Redhill took a long time, and every penny was needed to keep us, so her visits were few. Then she had a bad dream about George, and she felt she must go and see him. She found him in a bad way, his back covered with deep open cuts. He had been accused of stealing the Superintendent's gold watch, and had been birched before the whole school. After the birching, the other boys threatened to bind the real thief, who had not owned up, and put him on the railway line. The lad was terrified, went to the Superintendent and confessed his guilt. There and then the boy was sent to another school for his own safety. The Superintendent told Mother the whole story, and apologised.

This punishment, the harshness of it for something he had not done, made a deep impression upon George. Soon afterwards he ran away from the school, having served eighteen months. He escaped the police several times and managed to get work, but the climax came when he met a policeman face to face and thought he was about to be arrested. George was carrying his dinner plates; he hit the officer with them and got away. After this he went to sea.

A sad incident occurred soon after he had run away from the school. His suffering had left its mark, and it had also estranged him from his mother. After a serious talk from her he announced that he was going to leave home and never come back. Mother answered simply: "You'll want me, my boy, before I shall want you." He left, and Mother suffered horribly. Then, early on a bitterly cold morning, there was a knock on the door, and there was George with head hung low, the milkcan in his hand. He was broken and starving. Mother wept with joy, and of course took him in.

Another brother, Albert, a good looker, got into bad company. He drank, but it took little to make him drunk. Women adored him. He left home and sank into bad health and poverty. Mother never stopped looking for him, and at last found him and brought him back. He died in New Zealand.

Brother Will was perhaps the most charming of the family and the most gifted. He was among the very few who first learnt to sharpen and harden steel saws, and he could have done well for himself, but drink ruined him. I ministered to him at the end in the London Hospital and gave him two pints of my blood in the days when blood transfusion was something fairly new. It was strange to see blood giving him life and colour. Dear Mother went backwards and forwards in her old age to the hospital to visit him.

My eldest sister Esther was the only member of my family who was confirmed and went to church regularly when I was young—a baby in fact. She married an Australian merchant seaman, Frank Farrow. Sis, as we called her, was in very poor health for many years and died of T.B. at twenty-eight.

Mother and Sis were very dear to each other. When Sis was well enough to get up she did machine work at home, but that was not very often.

One thing burnt itself on my memory when my sister was very ill. The Blessed Sacrament was administered to her, and must have been brought straight from the High Altar of St. Saviour's through Hill Place Street to her sick-bed. I think it must have been Easter Day but I am not sure. There were two priests, both fully vested. They wore golden vestments with apparels, they may have been dalmatics. I hadn't seen anything like that before and I haven't seen anything like it since. I was very young, no more than six or seven, but I can see every detail now and I can see myself watching in the road as the two priests passed. That is how things were done at St. Saviour's, Poplar, over sixty years ago.

A picture of my sister has never left me. She seemed tall and thin. She had a lot of hair and a lovely speaking voice. Her face was always pale but lit up with two red spots on her cheeks. From a high and rather broad forehead her face tapered delicately and not too quickly to a pointed chin. Her eyes were blue. Sis was good. I used to think her holy. Her death was rather fine. She had a vision of glorious lights as she died. She had no fear of death.

Tom was four years my senior. He used to bully me when I was young and once he kicked me in the face, for which Mother thrashed him. He was the only one of us I saw hit by Mother. It was Tom who once nearly lost us a whole week's money. Clothes were pawned on Monday mornings, and if all went well they were redeemed on Saturday for Sunday. Mill's in Devons Road was a popular pawnshop in those days. It was a wretched business, for the interest on the loan did not alter but the clothes or boots aged and the amount allowed got less, so poor people got further and further into debt. Money was of great value then. Often a half-sovereign was all that came into the home on a Saturday, and every penny had to be carefully spent. Mother saw few half-sovereigns, for she was paid for each day's work and spent the money as soon as she got it. It was for very many years "hand to mouth" with us. One Saturday Albert gave Mother half a sovereign and she had no more. She gave him the shilling he would keep out of his money, wrapped the golden coin in a piece of newspaper and sent Tom to Mill's Pawnshop to get something out. Off he went over Stinkhouse Bridge and into Devons Road. Some time afterwards he returned in great distress; he had lost the half-sovereign. Mother could take shocks and keep calm. Tom was waiting for a thrashing, for he knew what it meant to Mother and to us all. When she said, "Come here, boy, and keep still," the kindness made him feel worse but she went on: "Now tell me how you went and where you stopped." So she catechised him. "You went round the corner by Mrs. Bardwell's sweet shop, you crossed the road and went over the bridge . . ." Then suddenly he flew off down the street, while Mother sat quiet and closed her eyes. She remained so, I think to pray, but perhaps to collect herself too, which could be the same thing. Before Tom got back to the door we knew he had found the coin. He had got as far as a sweet shop where he had stopped to do up his bootlaces—the laces of our tough cheap boots were always working themselves undone. The ledge of the sweet shop was wide and without a thought he had put the wrapped money on the ledge. His mind must have been wandering for although he went on automatically, he left the coin behind. It was strange that he should have so completely forgotten where he left it until Mother set his mind on the journey.

Losing money in those days was always a very serious thing, and the neighbours would all share in the search. There was never any question of anyone picking it up and keeping it. A stranger might do that but not a neighbour.

CHAPTER II

Schooldays

My first day at school stands out clearly in my mind. A crust of bread and a kiss was my breakfast as I ran across the road to the infants' school of St. Saviour's, at the age of five. When I got to school, there was placed before me a white mug of hot milk and a bun; it looked very big. I couldn't believe it was for me. I looked up, and there was a big fat man in black, with a funny hat on, looking down at me. He had a big face with a double chin; he was smiling; it was a lovely face. The man put his hand on my head and said, simply: "Eat." That was Father Dolling, and I think I have felt that touch ever since.

School meant nothing to me although I went regularly. In the infants' department I remember two things; the hot milk we had each morning, and Miss Wright, the governess.

Miss Wright was a motherly soul and most kind. She used to bring two little boys to the school on special occasions. They were very clean, beautifully dressed and I thought they were wonderful. I didn't feel jealous of them but I thought it would be grand to be like them.

At about seven years of age I moved up into the boys' standard. I don't remember learning anything at all. For the first four years my teachers were very kind, but the fifth standard master was a vicious brute. His name was Weaker and he was very thin and very sallow. When he used the stick, which he did far too often, his jaws worked in a curious and most ugly manner; it made him look like a wild animal.

When he called a boy out for punishment he waggled the cane and made it whistle, so to approach him was a nasty business. The stick was given on the hands, which was painful, especially in the winter when we shivered anyhow with cold in the classes. (Fires were rarely seen or felt, because the teachers placed themselves and their desks in front of them.) The temptation was to ease the hand away from the cane, but Weaker was an artist as well as a sadist and as he struck with the cane he brought it up like a whip catching the back of the hand or fingers.

I remember seeing his girl friend with him at our school camp at Broadstairs. She looked rather nice and I felt sorry for her.

To pass into the sixth standard was to jump out of the frying-pan into the fire, for Mr. Dan Neale was a terrible man. He was cunning. St. Saviour's being a church school, he used to toady to the clergy and keep in with them.

God alone knows why, but he was specially cruel to me, and I was caned almost every day for eighteen months. He could never make me cry and that made him mad. I should have thought more of him had he been cruel to all the boys, but he had four or five favourites who were allowed to cheek him openly and get away with it. Not only that, but he gave them gifts of sweets to curry favour with them when they sulked. I have wondered a thousand times why. Neale would bruise my hands with caning and then cane me again for bad copy-book writing.

When I was trying so hard after the First World War to get through an examination at Knutsford Ordination Test School, I went to see Mr. Matley, the headmaster of St. Saviour's. He looked at the maths paper and called Neale to his side. "Which of these did you find most difficult?" Neale asked. Although I was then twenty-four and had served over four years in the Army, I felt the same old fear of this man and limply told him of the problem. In the old sarcastic and sneering way he said, "One of my boys can do this in five minutes." But as soon as he began to write it on the board, I came to my real self and said I would give half a crown to the boy who got it right in fifteen minutes. None of them could do it. He knew that none of them could do it but he just had to try to humiliate me. He was furious at his failure. I then told him in front of Mr. Matley what a terrible brute he had been. My nephew sat in the front row and I told Neale that if he treated that boy as he had treated me I would crack him.

To go back to my schooldays. One of the many charitable acts of Lord Northcliffe (then Sir Alfred Harmsworth) was the provision of a summer camp for us at Broadstairs. It was said that, in or around the year 1900, Father Dolling sat on the doorstep of the Harmsworth Press until Sir Alfred saw him. The outcome of the resultant meeting was that Sir Alfred took 400 or more boys from St. Saviour's School to Broadstairs every year. The seven-year-olds went for a fortnight, the rest for a month. Our benefactor paid for jerseys, khaki suits, and band instruments. He hired forty tents and four marquees, with tent boards in each tent. He paid for twenty or more brakes to take us from school to Holborn Viaduct Station, and for a special train to take us to Broadstairs.

Our camp was laid out neatly in four rows of ten tents at the point between North Foreland Lighthouse and Kingsgate Castle by Joss Gap. There were Army cooks and we fed like the best.

I was the most miserable child in the camp when I first went to Broadstairs, although no greater care could have been taken of me. I was just ill with home-sickness and could neither sleep nor eat. That fortnight away from my mother was the longest two weeks of my life.

The other years, until I was fourteen, were good. Although I did little about them, there were numerous competitions for the boys, with prizes for the best collection of wild flowers, seaweed, sea-shells and the like.

Just what that camp at Broadstairs did for my health I did not know until very many years later. After the Second World War, I became very ill with some kind of lung trouble, and X-rays showed many scars on my lungs. The specialist asked me about my early life, as he said I should have been dead ages ago. He gave the opinion that Broadstairs and the food and air there had saved me.

When we were bigger we marched from Broadstairs station to the camp but first we skirted "Elmwood", the home of Sir Alfred and Lady Harmsworth. Our band played, we marched well. Bob, Sir Alfred's dog, was let out of "Elmwood" to come to camp with us for the month and in all my years at Broadstairs I can't remember one without him.

Our time was well planned. Reveille was at 7 a.m. at 7.30 we lined up and ran down Joss Gap to the sea, with Bob leading the way, to swim. Breakfast at 8, and how we ate porridge and bread and butter! Tons of it. After Grace, which we sang beautifully, the orderlies raced about 150 yards to the cookhouse for the porridge and the rest of the food. Prayers after breakfast were taken by the vicar or one of the staff of St. Saviour's Church.

After breakfast, we all prepared for tent inspection which started at 11 a.m. Prizes were presented for the best kept tent and marks were read out each night. I have been to many camps in my life but I have never seen anything to touch the spirit of smartness and cleanliness of that camp.

In the afternoon we were allowed on the beach. When the tide was out and the weather good, it was just heaven. It was a sandy beach and a bay in itself with rocks either side. The warm pools between the rocks had crabs, eels and shrimps and were loaded with winkles. We could only play with the crabs and eels but we took the winkles in our enamel mugs and got the cooks to put boiling water on them and we had a delicious tasty tea with our bread and butter.

After tea we had outdoor games, cricket, football and rounders, or there were evening concerts on bad weather nights, the boys always supplying the talent.

At about 7.30 p.m. we had cocoa and bread, notices were given out and then there were prayers.

The prayer that moved me more than any other in that great tent was "Visit we beseech Thee O Lord this camp and drive from it all the snares of the enemy; let Thy holy angels dwell herein to keep us in peace, and may Thy blessing be upon us evermore." Even now that prayer never fails to take me back to the Broadstairs Camp. The silence in the marquee during prayers was complete, although 400 boys or more from the age of seven and a half years to fourteen years were involved. We always sang, "Lord keep us safe this night; secure from all our fears; may angels guard us while we sleep; till morning light appears."

After prayers each Section leader took a hurricane lamp and led his family of nine off to his tent. Then, cuddled down, two or three sleeping together to be warmer, there were stories and chuckles. The lamps were put outside; the signal to be quiet was given when the officer came to collect the lamp. He said "Good night" and the tent answered with one voice, "Good night, sir." To hear those good nights all through the camp was very lovely. After that there was dead silence and sleep.

At the end of the month's holiday we had sports of every kind and for every age. On the final night we had a most glorious fireworks display lasting for an hour or more, and generally Sir Alfred and Lady Harmsworth joined us. We thought they were the nicest people in the world. Every one of us loved them. They had their photographs taken with us in a group and we were each given a copy.

One thing more this great man did. He gave us all a new half-crown for Christmas, which was a lovely present for Mother.

I went to Broadstairs seven or eight times.

Holiday Mondays at Blackheath Fair Ground were another treat to look forward to. As young as eight years old we would set out on the long walk from Poplar, through Blackwall Tunnel, a mile and a quarter long, shouting and singing and listening to the many echoes coming back at us from all directions: it was uncanny fun.

When we were in funds we might have twopence for the day. the height of our ambition was to win a coco-nut, and a penny would give us three balls to shy, and that, being children, from half-way. The Fair men and women were kind to children. If we managed to unseat a nut they would give us a broken one. We tried hard to save it until we got home, but hunger usually beat us and we would go shares.

We could take part in very few, if any, of the competitions, nor could we afford the roundabout, but we loved the noisy music and watching the fun. We never left until we were exhausted, and then there was the four or five miles back. We always tried to save a halfpenny for a bit of new bread on our way home. Bakers were always open, and a "ha'p'orth" of bread was a good lot. I can hear the kindly tone of my mother's voice now as we turned into Hill Place Street, for she would be at the door. Home is very lovely when you are tired and hungry.

I was weak and half-starved, yet I was tough. I once had a fight that lasted a week with the "clipping" bully of the school. He was bigger, fatter and fuller than I was. He would clip the ear, tap the ankle and keep boys caved down by cruelty. He clipped me once, and then again, and I tried to get out of his way, and still he came on. Then, although I was afraid, still I cracked him a beauty full in the face. I was saved by the whistle at the end of playtime, but I knew what must come. Signs were made in class and everybody was working up for the fight in the "square", the fighting place in Stainsby Road. Fatty "R", after school, demanded the square, and like a lamb to the slaughter I went. By his size and bounce I was nothing, and the supporting followers were all his. A few would have liked to see me win, but it was because they too had suffered under Fatty, not because of their liking for me.

As the fighters, we were crowded in. As we moved in to hit or to sidestep, so the crowd moved with us. This arrangement meant that the fight was a real fight; the contestants, often against their will, were kept close together.

I was very nervous at the start, for Fatty was reputed to be really hot stuff. There were no rounds—the thing went on until your arms were so tired that they would not keep up. So the art was to drop your arms for precious seconds as wild fists flayed by, and so to give them ease before driving them home again.

The temptation was to shut your eyes against threatening fists (especially for a youngster) and invariably you lost if you did. I learnt in that fight to keep mine open. I was steadied in the first exchanges by a crack or two in the face and body. I lost my fears and kept my wits, but I still expected to be put out. Nearly all the attacking was being done by Fatty, yet I felt a mounting elation, realising that I was learning to take it and to dodge it. My mind was alert and although I was hardly thirteen years old I was watching

C

the way he was working. He came in the same way every time and did the same things with his hands.

For about twenty or thirty minutes this went on, and we were both bleeding and getting tired. Then the shout of "Copper" went up, which nearly always ended fights in East London in those days. The police might appear in the course of their regular beat, or because they had been sent for. If you were lucky—or unlucky—you might have an undisturbed fight, for as much as an hour. Often it was a relief when the policeman came for the fighters grew exhausted and yet would not give in.

Our first bout was on Monday and we resumed the fight day after day until Friday. Although I got very sore, and it was difficult to keep Mother out of it, or to keep her from keeping me out of it, I gained confidence. A cut lip and a black eye was something when you were still on your feet and not minding the next session. The boys began to view me in a different light. Fatty was losing caste, and although he was still dangerous, for he was rushing in and often hitting harder when he landed, I knew I had him beaten if I could last. The police did their job night after night.

On Thursday I hurt my right hand badly, but got through all right. It was then that I learnt that my brother Albert had been watching me. I got home and my hand was painful and swollen. Mother was angry because I was fighting. Albert told Mother to let me alone and he looked at my hand and dressed it with cold water bandages. He then said, "You must beat him tomorrow night." It had, in fact, never occurred to me to think of the end of the fight, for until I hurt my hand I knew he could never beat me.

On Friday evening he came into me just as he had done the first day and I knew he had learnt nothing. So as he came in, I met him each time. His head went down and my left fist met his face dead in the middle and at last he could not go on.

As a result of this fight I gained in prestige and might have been a leader. But I was needed at home. And my appearance did not lend itself to leadership. I was small and skinny and I had a bad squint, which caused me a deal of trouble. I was often called

"Bosco" and I felt it. And I had to suffer even more from my schoolmaster Neale. Fatty was one of Neale's favourites and he did not like his favourites beaten.

Youngsters had little money in those days, but we had lots of fun; we made it. Football was the most popular game. The school playground was no more than 20 yards long and 10 to 12 yards wide. There was a wall about 6 feet high plus a bit of wire fencing to keep the ball in from the street; the other wall was the north side of the church—the church windows were protected by stiff wire. In this small space sixteen or more boys would play with a very small ball costing a penny or two. The speed and the roughness of the game made us dizzy, the passing and the accuracy of goalmaking was sheer artistry. We would play for hours.

That kind of football was superior stuff under the best of conditions. But think of that kind of football, daylight gone, the only illumination given from a badly mantled gas lamp-post. The area, the pavement, 2 yards wide and the length about 6 yards. The football a small stone no bigger than an inch any way. Two of us would play for a full hour or more. The width of the pavement would be the goals. We were so quick of foot that we would use the wall as a billiard player uses the cushion. If the opponent's legs were the slightest distance apart, the stone would be between them like a shot out of a gun. In that small place and in semi-darkness we would weave and turn round each other and the game was absorbing and rigorous.

Then there was "Say go" and "Kick-can-policeman", both hide-and-seek games. The hiding-places were plentiful, deep doorways, street gutters in which to lie full length, the canal bank, and lamp-posts up which we would climb.

Some games were a bit cruel. A favourite sport was to tie a farthing bundle of wood to a length of string, set it in the gutter when old people were passing and pull it away as they bent to pick it up. We would gain the curses of the old people as we ran away laughing. Or we would tie two knockers together in narrow streets where there was little or no lighting and then knock at one.

It was amazing how many times the people would open the door and curse before they realised what was happening.

A deal of fun was got out of pretending to wind up cotton. This was done when factory workers poured out of the works. One of us would sit on the curb and the other against the wall of the pavement. We just twiddled our fingers and said "Mind my cotton, please," and all the people hesitated and stepped high and it was just funny until the people realised what was going on and then we got a hit or a kick. A memory of this game came back to me, years later, when we were trudging through the mud to the front line on the Somme. The warning would come down the line, "Wire under foot," or "Wire overhead." My mind flashed back to my childhood, and wickedly I called out, "Wire under foot," and in the darkness I saw in my imagination hundreds of feet lifted high and hundreds of heads bowing to avoid the wire that wasn't there. It seemed funny to me at the time, weak and silly with fatigue, but I should have been in trouble had the others found out I was fooling them.

The most daring game we boys played was a sort of follow-my-leader known as "doing my Dads". Why it was called that I have no idea. Our leader in this hair-raising, dare-devil game was a boy named Tommy Anderson, and we had to do everything he did or we were considered poor fish and were shooed away. Some things he did were ordinary, like climbing a lamp-post and swinging on the arm which stood out from the old-fashioned lamp, but the most terrifying "dare" took place on the tow-path of "Lim'ous Cut". The canal is very deep, and the water was very low, and it was dark, when Tommy ordered us to lower him by his feet until his head touched the water. It needed strength and awkward teamwork to get him up. We could all swim like ducks, none of us would have drowned, but the "dare" had to be done as ordered and completed by the leader. To be upside down in the hands of others, to be lowered and dipped then pulled up took an awfully long time to happen and it was a sick-making business. Solemnly we all went through it, before Tommy chased off with us after him as he thought up what to do next.

We had elaborate games with playing-cards, buttons, and

spinning tops. The girls were expert at five stones, played with a round stone called a "bonce", and five square coloured stones called "gobs". And, thinking of girls' games, what joy it was to watch a dozen young girls of nine or ten years old dancing beautifully to the music of the barrel organ.

At the end of the long summer evenings we would sit round in a group telling stories, as many as fifteen of us, boys and girls. How I wish I could remember some of the stories now. The extent of the imagination was wonderful. Dick Sykes, the cripple boy, was the best story-teller, and I remember hanging on every word.

Though we had no money, and very little to eat, we made our own fun and we were very happy.

CHAPTER III

Poverty

I HAVE said school meant nothing to me; I learnt absolutely nothing. One reason for this I think was that I was always hungry. We were desperately poor but we were kept clean. In the eyes of those who should have helped us, poverty and cleanliness did not go together. The really poor and needy were to them the filthy ones. So that when Sir Alfred Harmsworth gave Mr. Matley, the headmaster, hundreds of pairs of shoes to give away, no Williamson child got a pair. I remember having a very bad heel and having to go to school on my brother Tom's back. Mother said, "Ask Mr. Matley if he could let Joe have a pair of those shoes." When Tom asked, Mr. Matley replied, "They are only for poor children." Our clothes were patched and repaired but we were not poor because we were clean!

There were free dinners for poor children but never for us. Even in those days I wondered why our family was not included for the free dinners, bought by and arranged by Father Dolling. The money he begged for came from people who had plenty and to spare. What family in Poplar suffered more than ours? The blackest day I remember was when five of us were left with half a loaf of very stale bread. It was winter and there was no fire. On this occasion we weren't thinking of ourselves but of Mother, for she had no work. We knew she was tramping the streets looking for work, which meant she was more hungry than we were. That evening she found a few bits and pieces of bread for us but things were very black and dismal. Her usually bright and cheerful face was deeply scored by hunger and distress. The occasion burnt itself into our memory and in later years Mother told us that for forty-eight hours she had had nothing but water and a raw carrot which she found in the gutter. She would not come home because she would have been tempted to share our half-loaf. Her clothes lacked warmth and her old spring-sided boots were worn and thin, and in these she walked and walked, pleading for work and food, but finding nothing but crusts of stale bread, and these she brought to us.

Our breakfast usually consisted of a slice of bread and margarine (fourpence or sixpence a pound) and a cup of tea just coloured with skimmed milk. Half a pint of "skim milk" cost three farthings and was left in small cans with lids on each morning. I used to feel as if I had got a hole in my body; my stomach ached with hunger. The vicarage cook, Mrs. Linguard, used to let Mother have a basin of dripping every Monday night, and my sister Doll had to go to the tradesmen's entrance of the vicarage to get it. That was in Father Dolling's time and in the early years of Father Trollope, sixty years ago. The dripping was from the vicarage Sunday joint.

Most midweeks we never had a meat and vegetable dinner; bread and "marg" was our fare. I well remember one bitterly cold day, when my feet were dead with cold, arriving home from school and kicking at the door (I couldn't reach the knocker). Mother opened the door but I was also met with the smell of hot stew. It was so unexpected and out of course that I shouted, "Oh, Mother, and are there dumplings?" There were! And onions and carrots and barley and lots of pieces of meat. The joy of feeling my feet belonging to me again and the natural warmth making my face burn hotter than my hands was wonderful The opposite was the rule. I came in from school with my sister and brother at noon to a bleak cold empty home; no fire of course. A lonely halfpenny or penny sat on the table with the bread. We then got a halfpennyworth of bread-pudding from the coffee shop on Stinkhouse Bridge, and a halfpennyworth of jam for the bread.

It is strange to recall now what conditions were like in East London in those days before the First World War.

Beer was very cheap and people could get drunk on about

threepence. Some beer was a penny a pint. Fish and chips could be bought for a penny. "Ha'penny and ha'p'orth" was what we sang out for in the fish shop, but minus the H's. Coal was cheap enough to get, seven pounds for a penny. Bread was around twopence a loaf and Mother bought it "stale" because it went farther. There was little or no help from the Board of Guardians, but there was always an invitation to the Workhouse, where, for married couples, it was the parting of the ways, since men and women were rigidly separated, no matter how long they had lived together.

I have often wondered why the local authorities dealing with parish relief were called guardians. Was it because they were guardians over the money, or were they supposed to be guardians of the poor and needy?

Undertakers were always busy. Men, women, and children died of tuberculosis called then consumption. There could not have been a better word to describe the kind of starvation which left people to live on nothing but their own flesh and blood. They wasted away and were consumed. Many East End babies died of hunger; father had no work, mother could not buy milk, and she had nothing to give of herself.

Father Dolling had a soup kitchen going in the Gerard Street Mission Room belonging to St. Saviour's. It was open at 5.30 in the morning so that men, looking for work, could have a basin of soup and a hunk of bread before they set out on the hopeless trek. Things were so desperate that labour could be had for next to nothing. Long hours were demanded and, if a man made the slightest objection, there were always plenty of others waiting to take the job under almost any conditions; driven to it by starvation. Mother said of one young married man, "He is dying on his legs," and that is literally how many a young man died, going on until he actually dropped.

If there had been work for all, many men and their families would still have died of starvation because the wages were so terribly inadequate. My brother worked over sixty hours a week for six shillings, getting a shilling a year rise if he was lucky. My sister Doll worked at Batgers the sweet factory, which is still in

Stepney. She got four shillings for a fifty hour week for the first year. She paid a halfpenny fare from Burdett Road to Stepney Station. Doll asked Mother if she could leave Batgers and learn machining, making shirts and trousers, but it would mean earning nothing for two weeks. Mother hadn't much faith in Doll's abilities but she made the grade. She did sixty hours a week machining skirts and trousers at piece rates, and the girls were sacked if they could not earn thirteen shillings a week. Doll never looked back and is, at the age of seventy, still an expert machinist. But the struggle to obtain and keep employment when she started was appalling. Men and women worked each other out of jobs and undercut the already scandalously low wages, rather than starve altogether.

I well remember two hawkers meeting and fighting; fighting for the trade of the area. It was Sunday afternoon and they were selling delicacies for Sunday tea—watercress, winkles, celery and some fruit. A hawker's round, like a doctor's practice, was saleable and one of these two hawkers should not have been there. Their barrows were pushed aside, the contents forgotten. They stripped to the waist and fought.

One was tall and slim but muscular; the other thick-set with huge shoulders and short powerful arms. From the crowded houses humanity poured out, for Poplar loved a fight. There were, of course, no rounds, no pauses to regain breath. The shorter man hammered away at the other's ribs and stomach, pink patches blazing up with every punch which went home with a dull thud. The tall man's target was the face and neck and from the short man's face blood poured and splashed.

They must have fought for an hour, one gasping for breath and pinched with the pain of his bruised and broken ribs, the other almost blind, his eyes closed and bleeding, his face a bloody pulp. Suddenly there was the cry, "Coppers", a diversion for which many longed, including, I think, the men themselves. The two men were hurriedly helped into their things and a bucket of water was produced into which both ducked their heads. They then walked unsteadily to their barrows, which had remained untouched, and shoved them away in opposite directions. Soon they were calling their wares and selling "penn'orths" of winkles and "'a'p'orths" of watercress two or three streets away. It took them hours to earn a shilling and their boots would be walked off their feet.

You got nothing that you didn't earn in those days and if you were in a job you earned more, much more, than you ever got.

The winters were terrible. Bed was the warmest place, but I can almost feel the shock of my brother Tom's cold feet now. It took us a long time to warm up. The sheets were poor, when we had them, and the blankets thin, and they were supplemented by very old coats. I had nothing like pyjamas and my thin day shirt was also my nightshirt. My knees, under my shirt, came up to my chin almost, and in that ball, when my legs and feet thawed a little, I slept. In the morning we were cold through. My clothes consisted of a cotton shirt, a coat which had no collar but lapels in the front, knickerbockers to the knee, cotton socks and generally very shabby, heavy, hard boots.

Mother's greatest worry was to keep boots on our feet, and she would almost plead with me not to play football because the boots were soon kicked out and they were expensive to buy. I couldn't keep from playing, and paid the price of having leaky boots. Our clothes lacked warmth, they had no guts to them. A coat curled up and shrank after rain. Our shirts were cotton and very thin at that. We never had overcoats nor, of course, raincoats: the first overcoat I had was from the Army in 1914. Even in school we shivered, for in bad weather we sat for three hours at a time in wet boots. The one fire was shielded by the big forms of the teachers, who burnt and scorched themselves and still wouldn't move. "Turning sides to middles" was a favourite expression of my mother's, and that was how she repaired our clothes. The seat of my knickerbockers would be out, and the sides of an older pair would be used to make a patch.

For many years Mother took in washing. In the winter months the great difficulty was to dry it. When a fire was lit it was surrounded by steaming clothes, and heavy flat irons stood in front of it to heat up, the drying being completed by ironing. Mother never stopped working on winter evenings and she would sing as she worked, in a strong, sweet, musical voice. I would sit in a corner unless I was playing out in the street, and watch fascinated as her strong arms brought down the big hot irons on the butcher's smock, for which, washing and ironing, she got threepence.

From ten years old upwards I helped her a lot, especially in collecting and taking home washing. When I got into the choir at St. Saviour's, Father Dawson got her the clergy washing which she loved to have. Taking big baskets of washing home in winter was the most painful operation. I wasn't very strong and I was thin and small. I would bravely lift the big baskets of beautifully clean and ironed clothes, just reaching the handles with my hands, but only just. Mother would stand at the door until I turned the corner. I had no gloves, of course, and it was the pain in my hands I felt the most. Sometimes it was a relief when they went numb. But I had more than my hands to think about. The basket would be moved from the ledge of one poor little hip to the other. When they were too sore to use any more I would use my knee, taking one step at a time. I could have howled with pain a thousand times, yet that half-crown that Mother would get was in the forefront of my mind. I mustn't drop or spill this pile of treasure or she would have to do it all again.

At last I reached Mrs. Warner's house. She would count the articles carefully and nearly always find something a little bit wrong. Sometimes she would say Mother had charged a halfpenny too much. Fearfully I would say the proper thing, though I knew her to be a sweating bitch. She would sometimes give me a halfpenny and I would nearly genuflect with gratitude.

But the change going home after relinquishing my load was amazing. I would sing at the top of my voice and run and play my arms like the car-men used to, first at full length and then bringing them across each other around the body. There is nothing so warming. The freedom from the burden was heaven.

There would be three or four journeys like that each week. Taking dirty washing home was child's play; the hard labour was with the clean.

Sometimes, instead of bringing the washing home, Mother would do it at people's houses. She went to a fishmonger named Brown every Monday, and got her dinner there and all their stale bits of bread, and half a crown for eight hours' work. The dinner, and the stale bread-crusts for a bread-pudding for seven or eight of us, were of considerable help. I remember her saying laughingly on one occasion that Mr. Brown, whom I remember as a grumpy, bullying old man, had looked into the wash-house and seen what his wife and daughters had set her to do, and in a loud voice had remarked: "That family of mine will kill you." "But," Mother added, "he didn't offer me another sixpence!"

A woman once sent for her to go and do a day's work for half a crown. Mother counted the articles to be washed and there were fifteen dozen. She plucked up courage to say, "No, I can't do it," and the woman, who had heard of Mother "singing while she worked," said, "You sing and work and you will soon get through it." Mother told her to work and sing and do it herself and went home. The woman's husband came round later and said, "Please, Mrs. Williamson, come and do the work and tell me what you think I ought to pay you." It took her two days and she received five shillings but he also sent her bread and cheese and half a pint of beer for her dinner.

How deadly dull and uncomfortable that sounds—little to eat, little warmth and poor shoes and clothing. Yet while Mother was about, life was never dull. She was an optimist, and she was very nearly always laughing, joking or singing. In the depth of winter she would be in the wash-house in the pitch-black of the early morning, with a candle for her only light. She wore an old pair of men's boots, she had a large doubled piece of sacking from her waist to within eight or nine inches of the ground, her sleeves were rolled up as far as possible to the top of her arms, her neck was open. Her near-black straight hair was well pinned so that it didn't snake over her face as she scrubbed the butcher's huge, dirty greasy smocks. I loved to be near her when I was small, even in the wash-house. She would say, "Go inside, boy, it's cold out here," but her company was warming.

This picture of my mother at the washtub may not seem attractive, yet she was always completely mistress of herself. She was full of common sense and understanding. She was so patient and kind to silly people: people who couldn't manage, or who were bad managers; weak people.

My great friend, Father Lambert, said once, "Your mother is one of nature's greatest ladies." She was that, for she detested cruelty and would suffer and sacrifice to prevent it. She loved the grace of lovingkindness for its own sake. She had uncanny wisdom; she never thought of herself, and she carried a terrific load of other people's sorrows and problems. Yet the yoke seemed to fit her and she carried it naturally and easily. She gave comfort in everything she said and did.

CHAPTER IV

St. Saviour's Church

WHEN I was first noticed by the Church of St. Saviour's it was because of my very good natural singing voice. It was a lucky day when I went to that children's Mass. I must have been about eleven. I knew nothing of the service except one hymn, and I don't remember what that was; but I knew it, and I sang it. After the service, a lady worker, Miss Duncan, a woman of the grandest character, Irish, cultured, humorous and utterly unselfish, took me by the collar up the middle aisle to Father Dawson, and said: "This boy can sing—put him in the choir." That landed me; I loved church, and I never missed a service when the choir was wanted, and we had such services in plenty.

At first I came in for the constant rebuke of Mr. Weller, the choirmaster. He was the headmaster of Farrant Street School, and in consequence the choir consisted mostly of his schoolboys. He never liked me, and I was sensitive enough to know that I was poorer than his boys, more ignorant and much lower in the social scale. I don't think he meant to be unkind. My voice was very sweet but very strong and it attracted people to me, but when they came closer they found me ill-nourished, cross-eyed, and generally unprepossessing. So Mr. Weller would say, "Keep your voice down, boy," and his boys and the men would glance at me reproachfully.

I might easily have left the choir after a short trial but I liked singing and there was one pair of eyes which gave me great encouragement. They belonged to Father Dawson. He hadn't a note of music in his make-up yet he appreciated my God-given voice, the one nice thing about me, and he stuck to me, and through me he came to know Mother. I think he not only admired my mother but he had a deep affection for her. He brought her work. He gave her his washing to do and she soon had the washing of all the staff of St. Saviour's.

He would arrive at our house with all sorts of material to be made up as curtains. I can see him now, his six foot odd of steel-like activity made clumsy by his over-eagerness to get on with the job in hand. Carrying yards of curtaining, much of it trailing behind him on the ground, he would reach our house, push open the door, and call: "It's only me, Mrs. Williamson, make these up for me as soon as you can, will you?" and down he would drop the pile and out he would walk. Mother would laugh and say: "What a fine man he is."

Many times through the years I have maintained that a true call to the priesthood is tested and shown in the power to love people who are unattractive or downright horrible. Anybody can like nice, clean, cultured people. But the terribly poor, the hungry, the weak, the ugly, the dirty, the ragged, the ignorant, those who can't talk two words of straight English, the prostitute, the criminal and the down-and-out; to love and to be sweet and good to such people is the sign of true calling. The Reverend Father Dawson had eyes and a heart for those who needed him and his like the most.

Being in the choir entitled us to a breakfast of bread and margarine and tea. I have forgotten now, but I probably seemed a bit of a pig as I dived for the food. Breakfast on Sunday mornings was at 7.15 at the vicarage, and needless to say I was never late. Mother was always up and I always went out like a new pin so far as cleanliness was concerned. One of Mother's many pointed sayings when people were dirty was, "Good Gawd, soap's cheap enough," which it was.

Our brand of toilet soap was "Lifebuoy", and it was very full of disinfectant, so strong that it made the flesh tingle like pins and needles; but I liked the clean smell of it, the smell of which I am reminded every time I visit hospital. It cost three halfpence for two biggish bars joined together.

I was not only clean and well groomed without but happy

within, even on the coldest mornings, when with the choir I knelt and sang through the most glorious Sung Eucharist. Nothing have I more longed for as a priest than the life and spirit of the people who presented themselves in large numbers Sunday after Sunday, at 8 o'clock at St. Saviour's. The word "glorious" summarises for me the uplift the Sung Eucharist gave me as a child, and I always want to go off the deep end when people complain, "It is a long time for children to kneel."

While grown-ups were receiving Communion, the choir sang at least two Communion Hymns, with a pause between each verse and a longer one between the hymns. Sometimes, and always at festivals, we had as many as four hymns before the last communicant returned from the altar rails.

What I loved more than anything else was the quiet dignity of my elders. The lines were long to the altar, where four priests administered the Sacrament. Some communicants knelt on the stone floor each time a move was made, others bowed right down. A frivolous or nervous grin was very rare and restricted to one or two of the newly confirmed.

I wonder if it ever happens now? In those days two well-built servers, in albs and apparels, after communicating, genuflected and stood on the nave-side of the altar rails, while the people knelt at the rails and departed. They were there to help the old people up and down and it was lovely to watch.

I was tough and I have always been tough and there was nothing sloppy about me. It was fitting, then, that it was while I was kneeling for twenty minutes to half an hour at such a service, that a voice spoke to me and told me I was to be a priest. It was the realest thing in St. Saviour's Church, Poplar, on that morning. It was more real than the people who moved up to the altar a foot in front of where I knelt and sang. The voice filled my being, and echoed through my empty, ignorant head. It made me dizzy, light-headed. It singled me out, isolated me, set me apart. It made me somebody.

Lost in wonder, carried away, I said even as I sang, "No, no, no." It just wasn't fitting. I hadn't a hope. I felt I was kidding myself, yet there was no explanation. I would not have entertained such a thought in my own stupid mind. I hadn't a thought like that in me. It might have been that I was exhausted and hungry, yet I was nearly always hungry. The voice and the message left me limp, but strangely peaceful for the rest of the service. I was carried through it on wings. I was out of myself, and it was meant to be that way. The call was a sweet reality which lifted me, rested me and held me.

The reaction afterwards, at home, was ordinary enough for a boy who felt with no regrets that there was nothing better than his own home, though he could have done with a bit more to eat, perhaps. It never entered my head that the call might have been a dream, because it just was not. What I did feel was a sense of shame that I should ever think of becoming a great man like Father Dawson or Father Mark Trollope. We East End lads looked up to our priests. I wonder if they realised their responsibility? What they said, we believed; what they did was right. They were on a pedestal, miles higher than anything I could hope to reach.

There were people who intruded into our lives out of curiosity, doing a bit of "slumming" as it was called. We smelt them out and they stank. But godly, gracious, true priests were wonderful in our eyes. That the priesthood seemed to be restricted to people who had class and education did not strike us as odd because we were used to it. That was how things were. But Father Dawson saw it was all wrong and began to hunt among East End lads for vocations to the priesthood. Nobody had taken notice of me, but God had.

I was just duff. I wasn't silly but I couldn't write, I couldn't say anything the right way round, I couldn't express in words anything I meant. My brain refused to function when put on a spot about anything. I was sensitive beyond measure. I floundered, felt unsteady and full of confusion when trying to make conversation. It excited and depressed me when I realised how ignorant I was. I looked at others with school satchels on their backs and hungered for their knowledge and ability. I longed to be at ease in speech. God had called me and it completely upset me. I couldn't tell anybody because I just hadn't the heart to

D

speak of it. It made me more dumb than usual. If I had tried to tell anybody and they had laughed or been sorry for poor Joe, I think I should have clumped them. I lived with the knowledge alone, and that was meant to be, and it was best.

Soon after this wonderful and disturbing experience I was prepared for confirmation by Father Dawson. The only lesson I remember was the one which dealt with sexual matters, and there was some tittering—but not much, for Dawson was not one to allow boys to get out of hand. It was at one of these lessons that he asked four out of the five of us if we ever thought about ordination. Details about pay and other matters were discussed. I was not even asked if I should like to be a priest. Which goes to show that you never know. As I have said many times, Father Dawson could not be expected to ask me. With my obvious limitations, any such suggestion would have seemed madness. Still, I nursed my secret and wondered if a miracle would happen or if I had been tricked!

My voice broke and I left school about the same time and it was very trying indeed. Whereas the majority of boys left the church at fourteen when they left the choir, it did not happen to me. Religion had become a very vital part of my life.

My mother saw something unusual in me and she would often say, "I will not stand in his light." What that meant can be explained by something that was said when I was about to be ordained deacon. An old parish nurse who knew me all my days said, "Well, well, well. Some goes up and some goes down." Being ordained was "going up", not to heaven, but in the social scale.

Mother would have been content had I never visited her again after my ordination. Like Hannah giving up Samuel, sacrifice would have been her lot, though, of course, for different reasons. She could not read or write and had a fear she might let me down by not saying or doing the right thing. She knew, and so did I, of cases of sons and daughters who had "got on" and become ashamed of their parents. On the other side, we knew of Mrs. T. who would search out her brilliant son when she was half-drunk and shame him, so that he gave her money to get away from his office. So Mother, determined not to be a drag on me, would never own me before others. Always it was I who had to seek her out.

It was tragic that the Church, which in its priests and workers should have been so close to the people, was regarded by the people as being so much above them socially. And even today our sense of superiority or promotion remains cock-eyed. The true priests, the truly Christian souls, rise spiritually as they become in heart and soul one with the people, with even the most revolting and horrible people, dirty, ignorant people, sin-scarred people, people dying of loathsome, stinking diseases. The test of my vocation is to be able to minister, without effort, to the worst I know. After saying all that, I must add one thing; that having risen to the heavenly heights of ministering to the one who needs me most I must not fall into the sin of pride, feeling myself to be a fine feller.

I loved my Church and all it taught. My regular confessions made me clean and free. The absolute forgiveness from God came through His priest after confession, and for me there could be no substitute for confession. The habit of absolute candour in the confessional, the freedom from concealment and the self-knowledge it brings can be of the greatest value to others in distress. I have had young men really distressed about their guilt, and before I have realised it I have found myself saying, "That happens to be one of my own weaknesses."

One of the big problems of being a priest is that people tend to think of us as being somehow different from ordinary people. When people come to me and almost take it for granted that I have never been tempted or fallen as they have, I always assure them that common people have common sins and temptations. To be candid about one's own sins and weaknesses, of the past or present, is a tremendous help to the person before you. Priests differ in their views, but for me, confession is sharing, and to share one's own failings can be a definite help to both parties. Men and women have said to me, so many times, "What's the use? I'm no good, I've had it. What's the use of trying?" I tell them, "The sins and temptations of all men and women can be placed in a very small circle. We are made alike in many ways, and included in our common likeness are our sins and difficulties." Sex, selfishness and pride—even pride in the depths to which we have sunk—are common to all normal humans, and I am among them. We must meet them with courage and shame, with simple sorrow, and with determination to be better. This is the way I have found worth while, and I have found it through prayer and worship and confession—not a public parading of my sins, but private confession to God before a priest.

But all this was to be in the future. The present was a poor time for me. Schooldays were over and I had no job, little ability, and no special qualifications. Anything might have happened to me then. I had courage, but I had no money, no work, and was undernourished. Day after day I played around with another boy. That summer was my first year without a Broadstairs holiday. The St. Saviour's lads who did not go to the church school, and those who had left school, had an opportunity to go to Witnesham, a village near Ipswich. There was some payment to be made and the fare had to be found. For me that was impossible. Somehow I seemed to be the only one left behind and I remember feeling the loneliness of it all.

Then Father Dawson came to my rescue again. He had scarcely a bean, but somehow he begged my fare or gave me some of his very meagre pay. He came to Hill Place Street in a great rush as usual. "Bunter," he called, "come to Witnesham. I'll see you off to Ipswich and you can foot the rest." Mother had nothing to say in the matter.

I was called Bunter because like Billy Bunter in the "Magnet" I wore glasses. It might have been for the additional reason that, while I wasn't a pig for food like Bunter was, I was very nearly always hungry. But most unlike Bunter, I was never fat and, in fact, always very thin.

Off I went to Ipswich, arriving there late in the evening. Looking back, I only remember approaching the bell tents at dead of night almost exhausted. I woke everybody up and Alf Legrande called, "Come on, Bunter, turn in here." I took off my boots and jacket and fell asleep in the warm and welcome tent.

When I came back home from Witnesham Father Dawson had a job waiting for me. I was to go to Radlett as a page boy. When he took me off from Hill Place Street Mother shed a tear and said I looked like Oliver Twist, with my bundle under my arm.

CHAPTER V

First Jobs
and Growing Up

MANY things stick in my mind during my six months in service. The one great thing about it was the food—they fed me well. My first morning there caused me great distress. The cook, who sat like a queen at the head of the servants' table, was a tyrant. She was big and fat and she wore a stiffly starched, lengthy, voluminous pink dress, a white cap and a big well-starched apron. We had porridge for breakfast followed by bacon and fried bread. I had never seen such a spread. There was in front of me a pile of bread and a dish of lovely butter. That dish of butter was my downfall. I took some of it and a piece of bread, so that I had bacon, fried bread and more bread and butter.

"Boy!" said the cook, with a hell of a scowl on her face, "Do you have bread and butter with your bacon at home?"

I had never before in my life had bacon nor butter nor anything else on that table, except bread and tea. The reproach of that hard, unfeeling woman, with the looks of the footmen and maids, not forgetting the almighty butler, finished my appetite. My very guts ran away from me as my head hung and tears flowed. That was one of the very few instances in my life that tears had their way. None of my tormentors wished to be cruel; they just didn't know my life. To them I was just a pig, an ignorant pig from London. They were all country born and bred to service, and were tied to it by little money and good food and clothes.

On my first day I was wakened at 6 o'clock on a coal-black winter's morning. Unlike the house staff I had a bed with the outside workers, the cowman and such. Their barracks, clean and stiff with ice, was half a mile from the house. I ran through the darkness in this strange land. Then for an hour or more I filled and carried from an outside shed huge iron scuttles of coal. I could manage them no other way than to stand the rims on my knee, go forward with that leg and bring the other one up to it. It was hard and painful. Before breakfast I had to wash again because I was full of coal dust. How I wanted that breakfast! And the fool of a cook told me what she would do with me if I sulked, when in truth I was heartsick, hungry and tired, with a swelling on my knee that throbbed like a machine.

I got used to things, however, and loved the regular meals. Like my mother, I hate cruelty. I hate it partly because I have suffered it. A most cruel thing was done to me nearly every morning by the horrible cowman. I never got to bed before 10 or 10.30, and I dropped off to sleep as soon as my head touched the pillow. It was the cowman's job to wake me. There was a big old-fashioned iron stove in the ice-cold building, and he would lift me from my warm bed and sit my bare bottom on the cold iron plate. The shock of it nearly maddened me and the knowledge that it was coming haunted me. Cold administered like that while asleep is like being burnt. What fun it gave him, and how he had to pin down my arms to save his face from being torn open.

In spite of the hard work I grew strong. But after six months—I don't know why—I was sacked. I experienced no kindness at Radlett, but thinking back perhaps it wasn't their fault. The servants were ladies and gentlemen. I was a raw Cockney ruffian. I had no manners.

One other incident I well remember. I used to work very late because the gentry had their dinner late. One evening when I was alone and packing the dishes and plates which came through the hatch as course followed course, there came through what I thought was a lovely browned piece of fish. It gave me an appetite and I scoffed it. It turned out to be a delicious chop, but no matter, it was good. What I did not know was that Eric, the big fat son and heir, pride of his mother, had enjoyed his one or two chops so much that when he espied the last unwanted one, about to go through the hatch, he said, "Mumsie, I think I would like that chop for my breakfast." "Yes, darling, you shall," said Mumsie. Thus the butler, the footman, and the waiting maid, all waiting at dinner, were made aware of the desire for a meat breakfast by the son and heir.

Nobody missed the chop until the next morning. Much happened in the very early mornings before breakfast was served for the high and mighty. I had been sat on the cold stove by the bullying cowman to give me the usual shock to wake me. I had walked up to the house in the dark. I had lugged in the coal. I had washed and had a good breakfast. I had long forgotten my secret and delicious feast of the night before. After all the ten or twelve servants had turned each other inside out, and Mumsie had said her piece to all of them, the butler thought of me. I still hadn't an idea of what was going on, and I had even then a row of boots to wash as well as to clean; furthermore the old boss had ordered his best business boots to be returned to me because a cake of dry mud had escaped my attention. Looking very pale and worried, the butler came to my boot-room and asked, "Have you seen a chop, Joseph?" "A chop?" I repeated, and shook my head as I scraped the offending mud-cake, and wondered why people were so fussy. The butler went away and it was then that my guilt struck me. I very nearly ran after him, not so much to confess, as to find out more. I learnt all in time. Fortunately, it was thought that Mr. Eric's dog liked that chop too.

I felt no sorrow for my theft. I belonged to the house, I had worked since the morning's rude awakening for fifteen hours, and still was working; and I was hungry. Also I didn't like Mr. Eric. He was spoilt, he was big and fat, he always dragged his great feet and talked loudly so that the staff felt their place. He threw his weight about.

Sad to say, when I got back to Poplar I was terribly homesick for the country. I just couldn't talk and I couldn't sleep. I missed my clean bed. I missed the good food. I was most unhappy.

My depression was short-lived, however, for I was soon in the thick of church life and the activities of our wonderful club. The club was Father Dawson's, and I don't ever remember the vicar visiting it or the other two priests even looking in. There were two small rooms upstairs, with a small billiard table in one of them. Downstairs was a "run-in" from the road. The entrance was by way of a small door. The room had a very rough uneven floor.

The club was always very full. We paid a halfpenny a week. In the billiard room the crowd surged to get out of the way of the players. The billiard table had to be booked and each couple played for twenty minutes. The other room was used for smaller table games and for talking. Father Dawson generally sat and had fun in this room. His fun was sometimes very tough. In a twinkling he would have the strongest of us across his knees and spank us. The more we fought the better he liked it; he was like granite and we worshipped him because he was such a man.

Downstairs we boxed continually in a cloud of dust. I loved boxing, and hardly an evening went by for me without a good half-hour with the gloves on, and nearly always with the same lad. In John Bonner I had a boxing partner who was a head taller, several stone heavier and a year or two older. He could hit and I could take it and I could hit him as hard as I liked without any fear of breaking him up.

Through Father Halse (later Archbishop of Brisbane), I went to work at Wm. Cubitt & Co. in Grays Inn Road for five shillings a week. For this I rose at 5 a.m. six mornings in the week and arrived home five evenings at 7 p.m. and on Saturdays at 2 o'clock. For a year I was an office boy. There was another boy and together we swept the fifteen or more office rooms and did all the chores under a nice but bullying old man named Southgate, who himself worked like a slave. We answered two systems of telephones and ran messages.

My fares travelling to work cost ninepence a week. The tram conductors were grand men, they knew all the passengers and their destinations. Coming home at night nearly everybody would fall off to sleep after giving up the return of the workmen's ticket, and when I did this never did the conductor fail to shake me at Burdett Road.

My work was meant to lead on to a clerk's post in the office or into one of the shops as an apprentice. It was a poor show for me. The second year I went into the carpenter's and joiner's shop. I made glue for the men, and brewed their tea, and was generally the "kick-about" for all. A french polisher nearly killed me in that shop. He was a heavyweight boxer and one day without warning he punched me in the stomach, and I dropped. He and another man worked frantically on me to get my breath back. They were terrified. It was a great lesson for him. He must have been sixteen stone and I was the odd six.

Having no urge to become a carpenter, nor the money for tools, I was passed on to the engineering fitting shop. There, for weeks, I filed great lengths of T-irons, working with caliper gauge and template. At that time concrete poles were being made, and Cubitt's manufactured a contracting device for which my nine hours a day filing for five shillings a week played their part. Another unending job was filing to fit copper catches for small outside drain sinks for Peabody Buildings.

I didn't enjoy my Cubitt days; I worked, but my mind was not on my work, and I was very ignorant. For a long time I went to evening classes but I was too tired to take anything in, and going short of food was no help.

Outside work, there was plenty of excitement. The dances at St. Saviour's were wonderful. I could dance well and I would join in every dance from 8 to 11 o'clock. We had all the old "set" dances, but I think I liked the waltz best, because I loved the art of reversing. I was a bit small and young to partner adults, but I was always welcomed and well patronised. I enjoyed the coffee and cakes at these functions.

Before I was fifteen I was nearly driven away from church altogether. We have heard a great deal recently about "sending people to Coventry". I first learnt of this dreadful practice from the "Boys' Weekly" paper, the "Magnet", when Billy Bunter was ignored and left alone for hogging and spying and lying. I didn't think very highly of the practice then, and thought even less of it when I suffered it for three weeks, and was very nearly beaten by it.

It was this way. If we were at church on Sunday mornings we were allowed to use the St. Saviour's playground after the service. We always played football with a sixpenny rubber ball. The sides varied from six to eight or even nine a side. There was little room to move or run, and the game was very fast; it depended on quick timing, passing and fast shooting. The play was carried on within four walls in an area about 7 by 12 yards. Being Sunday, we had our best clothes on, and I had on my first decent suit, a poor thing of blue serge, rough material with little guts in it. But Mother got it through the "tally-man" at so much a week, and if things got very hard at home it would go to the pawn shop to bring in a few shillings.

In the course of play, down I went in my new suit, fell on one knee, and the poor stuff split. I thought I had been tripped up from behind and I sprang up and punched the offender, giving him a black eye. All might have been well had he turned and given me one in return, but he didn't and he wouldn't. He was older and bigger than I, and I had always thought him a better fighter. Also he was much more popular than I with the rest of the church lads, who were in full sympathy with him and furious with me. I was sent to Coventry from that Sunday dinnertime. My two particular friends would neither talk nor walk with me that evening. Instead of going out with them after church, I went home, very miserable. On Monday night I called at the club and tried to say I was sorry, but everybody ignored me. I offered to fight the boy when his eye was better, or to fight anybody he nominated. Still no response. The great Father Dawson did all he could to right matters but he couldn't move the lads. I somehow stuck to the club, where nobody would talk to me or play with me, and I kept to the church. For three weeks to the day I was completely ignored and unwanted. I could not doubt that the boys all wanted to drive me from the club and church, and there can be no doubt at all that they would have succeeded had they not at last given way.

Recently I asked my special friend of those days what made him and another friend come to Hill Place Street that Sunday evening. He could not remember, though of course he remem-

bered sending me to Coventry. I asked him to try to remember
why it was called off; he couldn't. My own view is that Father
Dawson did something, or was going to do something, to stop it.
When George Goldthorpe and George Compton called for me
on that Sunday night I went with them because Mother told me
to. I was completely broken in spirit and was unable to talk the
whole evening.

Not long after that, the vicar, Mark Napier Trollope, was made
Vicar of Birmingham, and that really meant the parting of the
ways. As lads, we had no influence at all, but we thought that
Father Dawson would be Vicar of St. Saviour's. The living was
in the gift of the Rector of Poplar. As I look back I can only feel
deep resentment towards whoever the Rector of Poplar was in
those days. Dawson simply must have been considered, but must
have been turned down for his politics.

I don't think I have ever met a man like Dawson. He was
cultured, a scholar, a brilliant conversationalist who could shine
in any company, yet he lived as one of the ordinary East End
people in an ordinary East End house. He had difficulty in con-
trolling his temper, especially when he met bullying. He always
kept order though, and was respected by all. He cared nothing
for money; he had little, yet was most generous. He was humble.
He saw nothing in me except that I was a very poor East End boy
with a soul to be cared for. I loved him because he was so naturally
kind to me and friendly to my mother.

He was turned down as Vicar of St. Saviour's and was allowed
to go to Australia where he was never happy. He came back to
England and had to start from scratch.

I would like to have seen him made Vicar of St. Saviour's. It
would have been nothing much to offer anybody, although for me
the fact that Father Dolling had touched the parish made it holy
ground. Better still, I would like to have seen him made Bishop of
Stepney. He would have been equal to the task for he loved and
touched the people of Poplar as Dolling and Wainwright did, but
he had scholarship also and a great power with the pen and tongue.
I saw most of his ability and looked up to him when I was a very

poor Poplar boy. I look back now and know that very often our Church dignitaries are bad or mad or just plain stupid.

Having said all that, it is most unlikely that I should have been ordained had Father Dawson been Vicar of St. Saviour's.

The rector sent Bishop Powell to be vicar and very soon a young married priest came as assistant. His name was William Noel Lambert.

He was quite different from the clergy under Trollope, and was not liked. Stupidly, many of the club lads hardly spoke to either Bishop Powell or Father Lambert because they felt that they were responsible for Father Dawson going.

I felt sorry for Father Lambert, and a handshake and a word sealed our friendship. I had been to evening classes and I had a drawing under my arm. He took it from me and asked me what the drawing was. As usual, I had gone through the classes and even done the drawing without knowing much about it, for I was tired and hungry. I think Father Lambert saw I was hungry, and after club he walked me to the vicarage. A large dish of fruit was a revelation to me; never before had I seen such a varied pile of lovely bananas, apples, oranges, grapes. In Gilson's, the green-grocer at the bottom of Arcadia Street, oranges, when they had them at four or six a penny, were very, very small and very sour, and apples were in the same category, very green and very small. In the Crisp Street market they might be a bit cheaper but of the same quality. The fruit at the vicarage was something different, and Father Lambert said, like Father Dolling some years before, "Eat." I looked at him as I had looked at Dolling, wondering if he meant it. I ate a banana and an apple and they were delicious.

Father Lambert's attention gained me the horrible and bitter name of "crawler" for a time. I cringed under it and temporarily avoided him. He cared for me because I was very, very ignorant and on the lowest poverty grade in Poplar. Nearly all the boys at St. Saviour's Church came from Farrant Street School, and they were the pick of the bunch. Very few indeed came from the Church School of St. Saviour's, although the Parish staff came into school to say prayers and teach most regularly. So most of the other lads came from better and more fortunate homes. I didn't resent it, I just felt the world was like that, and I used to find myself wishing, just wishing, that I could be like them, so that I might be comfortable and acceptable as they were to the priests of St. Saviour's.

As I look back, I remember longing to do something spectacular to make them see I was somebody. I tried it once, and it was the wrong way and the wrong thing to do. Four of us used to go for a walk up Burdett Road after Evensong on Sundays. We stopped at Tommy White's shop to buy some cheap chocolates. In the body of the shop was a picture postcard stand. I hoped to pocket one and show the other lads how smart I was. I got caught and was openly shamed, but it was the best thing that could have happened.

One of my earliest lessons from Father Lambert was his complete trust in me. He sent me for errands and gave me the money so that there must be change, and for some time I kept some of the money back. For a time it became a habit, then suddenly I realised how very terrible it was. He never spoke of it, and I believe it was because I always expected him to say something that I realised to the full my guilt. In one of my first sermons before him in Poplar I spoke of stealing his change. It wouldn't be right if I didn't say I paid him back with interest.

What he saw in me I cannot think. I was about fifteen when he came to the parish. My squint worried him and proper glasses put that right. He had a length of good serge cloth sent to him and he had it made up into my first decent suit.

What bound us more closely was trouble. I went to a Trafalgar Square rally to see Sylvia Pankhurst and hear her speak after one of her hunger strikes. I hadn't gone for trouble really, but in a scuffle over the police handling of the women I hit a policeman with an ash walking-stick. I could run, and the chase was on. Down Whitehall I went and the stupid crowd, instead of swallowing me up in its mass, opened up and made a passage for me. I dashed into what I think was Whitehall Gardens. I hoped there might be an exit as well as an entrance, but there was nothing but a high wall all the way round and it seemed as though all the police in London were after me. I was caught, I was beaten and run in.

I spent half a miserable night in a cell with the most lousy and loathsome people possible; they were terrifying and they were rotten in speech and in behaviour. The police looked at us through a slot and seemed to enjoy my fear and discomfort. To put a young lad in with people like that was most shocking and horrible. I knew the worst of Poplar but it didn't contain people like that, and my inside nearly left me both ways. I was terrified. There were four men in the cell; they stank, they spat, scratched, cursed, made as if to hit me because I wouldn't talk. They made filthy suggestions. To try to get out of it I banged at the peep hole and told the officer I wanted the lavatory. That officer was in keeping with the contents of the cell and I was pushed back with a curse from him.

Well into the night there was a great call from a cultured woman, "Are there any men who have been run in from the Trafalgar Square demonstration?" I shouted my name and I was bailed out, arriving home at 3 o'clock in the morning, very sore and bruised, to meet a very distressed mother.

I appeared in Court next morning. A policeman with a very swollen face and a black eye gave evidence against me and held up my stick, saying: "This is what 'e 'it me wiv, your 'onour." He left out the H's. After that I was the joke in Poplar. Everybody who knew me called, "This is what 'e 'it me wiv, your 'onour."

The magistrate gave me no time to answer the charge. He said, "Forty shillings or a month." Father Lambert came to see me at once. He said, "Do you want to do the month?" He paid the fine and I was free but not at all well, for I had been thoroughly beaten. I was lectured by him and from all sides about my violence and the fine.

A fortnight after my unfortunate downfall the suffragettes advertised a great public meeting at which Miss Annie Kenny would speak. It was to take place at the London Pavilion and Miss Annie Kenny had been freed from prison after her hunger strike and was due for re-arrest. It was a challenge to the police, which they took up.

In a weak moment, but from more than empty curiosity and some admiration and sympathy, Father Lambert took me to the Pavilion. I was quite determined not to get mixed up in a fight. After one or two speakers, Miss Annie Kenny appeared as from nowhere and so did the police. She was truly manhandled and in a moment I was chasing down the steps after Father Lambert. He went straight into the fray and into the inescapable hands of the police. As he was taken to Vine Street Police Station he called, "Joe, don't let them photograph me." Dutifully I pushed camera men and cameras from the path and I won through. The next day there was one picture of the "Rev. Miller", with his hat over his face.

I hung around the police station, not knowing what to do for the best. I got tired and worried and approached the Station Sergeant. Luck went with me, for in reply to my request to see the clergyman the Sergeant said, "Do you know the Reverend Miller?" However, before I could get to him he got to me, and he was free until the next morning. Like his protégé he got forty shillings or a month, the only difference being that he was freed without bail; I think they were glad to get rid of him. It was a little strange that we should both fall into the same trap.

My arrest and beating made a change in my life. I left Cubitts, the builders, because a Scots lady who was a suffragette thought it would be nice to educate me. Father Lambert urged me to go to this middle-aged spinster's house at Southminster. There was an oldish lady companion living there, who at once saw that she might get something less if I got something more.

I can remember little reason why Miss Mc . . . should have got rid of me so soon. Within a month or two she had written to Father Lambert to say, among other things, that I was "scatter-brained". I did odd jobs, but she made no suggestions as to how I might learn. The atmosphere was peculiar. It was winter and she had no heat in the place except an old closed-in combustion stove. We sat round it and after the early nightfall we could see only to get about, for the oil-lamps were very poor. I remember so well wondering what she wanted to do with me. As in winter in Poplar, the warmest place was bed, and one morning Miss Mc . . . opened my door and found me reading in bed. That seemed to be the end of her plan for me. She wrote to Father Lambert a letter expressing disappointment and full of complaints about me. She was an educated woman of sixty odd years. I think she must have expected something quite different when I arrived; probably a more educated lad and closer to her own set. What was difficult for me was keeping conversation going. She said nothing, so that when I gave up trying to talk, there was absolute silence as we looked at the iron stove which warmed our fronts and starved our backs with cold.

She sent me to a friend of hers a few miles away; a young widow with a little girl. I was shown a bed in a room in a big empty house, half a mile from the cottage. It would have been better had Miss Mc . . . sent me back to Poplar directly instead of passing me on to somebody else. It was an aimless waste of time and I was glad when I returned to Poplar. Changes came but no chances. I had gone away with the hope of learning something; I returned as I left, except for a more jaded outlook. Through all this I stuck to the Church and my church duties.

On my return to London I got a job at the Civil Service Stores in the Haymarket. It was in the chemist's stores department. I washed bottles, tried to learn names of drugs and things and ran errands for special drugs. It was a most boring job, amongst boring and wealthy people. I went to work on a bicycle and had two very near shaves. In Aldgate, on a slippery wet morning, the wheels of my cycle got into the tram lines and I fell under a bus and came up untouched, to the surprise of all witnesses. The second was much more spectacular. A great newsprint paper van was going up Fleet Street to a news office. It was drawn by four horses and to get up Fleet Street the horses had to zigzag. The speed of those horses was truly amazing. Thinking I should be able to overtake and get round them I pressed on with all speed on my bike. Too late, I saw a bus coming down Fleet Street with the turn of the horses. With the bike I must hit the bus, and go

E

under it or under the big horses now spreading themselves to the full to make the hill. I let the bike go, put my hand as far over the horse's back as I could and hung on. I stuck and went up to safety but my cycle was smashed to bits.

The only other incident worth recording in that job was winning the Stores' mile race. Father Dawson had left St. Saviour's a year ago, but during the eight years he spent in Poplar he had us all running. He was a Blue and an Olympic runner. He ran to keep himself fit and to teach us to enjoy physical fitness. When he left, a few of us used to go to the Victoria Park Cinder Track. A particular friend of mine, George Goldthorpe, worked at *The Times* newspaper offices, and *The Times* sports and my Stores' sports were about a month apart. He entered for the mile race at *The Times*, and I for the Stores'. We were both thought to be quite mad to run in such company; nearly all the runners were members of clubs. We were not much more than sixteen. At Victoria Park we were fortunate, for a professional runner called "The Blue Streak", whose particular training was for an hour's race, was training there. He was kind to us when we told him our aim. He told us we must run the mile in five minutes. I have forgotten how near we came to that, but he used us to help him. He would be going for twenty minutes, and we would let loose to do a mile, giving ourselves half a lap start. He would, of course, catch us up but then he would take us with him and that was grand.

I could not go to *The Times* event, but George came in second. When the Stores' day came George was with me. I went off like "The Blue Streak" while the other runners were shadowing each other and waiting for me to drop out. I was well out in front at the half-way and Goldie, my friend, did a bit with me inside the arena so that he could tell me what the hopes were. He was laughing and all he said was, "You must win if you can keep up your pace." Childishly, I said, "I can easily." The next lap Goldie was in fits of laughter and I was going well, with plenty left. It was wonderful to see the other runners bunched up, wearing their proper running shoes and club colours, nearly half a lap away. Yes, I was a good winner and I enjoyed it to the full.

The great shield was put up for the first time in the chemist's department of the Haymarket stores, with my name on it as winner. The bottle washer and errand boy had done his stuff.

I did not get through my teens without falling in love. If the lads hadn't a girl at the age of fourteen and onwards then they pretended they had. Although the term "tart" is used today to describe a prostitute, it was not always so. In East London, until at least thirty years ago, it was simply the name given to your girl friend. A friend of mine, who developed into Wm. Cubitt & Co.'s leading staff carpenter and joiner, was a Poplar cockney of the most amusing sort, with an accent and dialect that could not be understood easily by anybody west of Aldgate. At our Monday night club he bustled in and Father Lambert was sitting surrounded by many of us. Art, as we called him, said, "D'yer-see-me wi' me tart las' night, Faver?" To have a "tart" was being really grown up.

Rarely though did we go out alone with our girls. The boys used to be together and the girls together; then we would stop and talk and one of the girls would say something, titter, and run away and her particular boy would run after her and catch her and, on occasion, kiss her, but only seemingly against her will, though she never protested.

If ever a boy was in love, I was, and she was the queen of my heart. I am quite sure that had it not been for Father Lambert and an uneasy feeling that I was meant for the priesthood, I should have married that girl early in life. My future then would have been like this. Having a wife and a family and a job, if I had been lucky, at twenty shillings a week, we should have had one room at half a crown a week; then two at five shillings, then a house, if I could have afforded it, for eight or ten shillings a week. I should have brought children into the world and watched all but the very fittest die, for only the fittest survived. I should have lived as my mother had. One room of 9 feet by 6 would be a good sized room for Poplar. There would be one window about $2\frac{1}{2}$ feet square. The room would be upstairs, so that water would have to be brought. The water closet for the house would be in the very small yard, so that during the night in cold weather, or in case of illness, a bucket and pot upstairs would serve for all purposes. Windows were more often shut than open, although my mother was an exception in this, and would never have them shut; she was often thought to be a bit mad in consequence. There is, though, no coldness like coldness with hunger; and hunger was the rule and not the exception in Poplar in those days. One room would still be big enough until the third child arrived, for the second would nearly always be in bed with Mum and Dad. Number one would have a bed made up on two chairs by the big bed.

The bliss of marriage would consist of having a bed of modest size, 4 feet 6 wide, a table of, say 2 feet by 3, three chairs of 18 inches square. Oh, I should have had a job, and so we would have a bit of fire, but no fireguard. With the queen of my heart and two children, and with about 3 feet square to do everything in, including cooking, washing and just trying to sit, the bed would be the answer. And indeed until the kids were old enough— about three years old—they would be fixed on to that bed and with every excuse they would yell and yell. I would have come home tired and hungry after ten hours or more at work and the queen of my heart would have said, "I got yer a nice pair o' kippers, Joe, they was only a penny a pair. 'Old the baby a minute while I cook 'em. Be careful, she's wet again."

Should I have tired of limiting myself to a room or two if the family grew? Should I have been tempted, with the queen of my heart perhaps, to get drunk once a week, or even twice?—for to forget self and surroundings would only cost a bob. There were those who said the shortest way out of Poplar in those days was to get drunk. But who wanted to be out of Poplar? Poplar was home, and enjoyment at the pub was part of it. Hunger could be forgotten in drink. Those houses of joy were open until 12.30 a.m. and, especially at week-ends, shrieking went on continually, for against the singing conversation was impossible unless carried on in a high screaming note. For poor children there would be the long hours of loneliness, their sleep cut short by adults as they swung into a deafening popular song. It would be sung and sung again, until all were drunk, with song if not with beer. Twice drunk and three times drunk, as the song made the heads giddy and threw everybody into a frenzy of dancing. That was the height of joy and forgetfulness.

Such a frenzy quite often ended with women pulling at each other's hair and clawing each other's faces, rolling over each other in the gutter and roadway, while men were fighting. Or, drink being too much for me, I might have been carried home and dumped on the bed. Two hours later I would bestir myself to ease my need to find, in my more sober state, the queen of my heart in the arms of another man on the landing. Then the fur would fly. There would be another fight, my queen would see to my wounds and it would be bed and forgetfulness. Such was likely to have been my way of life had I married in early years.

Or it might be winter, when pubs had good fires. The singing and the dancing would be as before. But at "Time, gentlemen, please," the people would try to move off from a blazing hot pub to freezing cold to find they could not stand in the frozen streets. Down everybody went, not to rise again, and most would crawl home on all fours, men and women overpowered with hysterical laughter. All the pain would be felt in the morning.

You might well ask, what about the children? Most of them slept, woke and cried and slept again in their wet things. Sensitive children suffered. Some as young as five would be haunting the doors of the pubs calling to their drunken mothers or fathers. A sponge cake might be bought and taken to them and washed down with a sip of beer from mother's glass. Some youngsters would just cry, having tried in vain to keep the younger babes quiet. Some would be punished for crying and sent back home. Yes, the adult way of escape in Poplar was devilish hard on the dear children.

There were, of course, the sterling people who watched every penny and kept sober and decent. It was hard on such people when their children grew up and fell in with the majority.

My mother was tempted to drink and forget her troubles, but very rarely did she respond to the calls of people in funds. When she could afford it she had half a pint of beer with her bit of bread

and cheese supper and in winter she would put the hot poker from
the fire into the beer. She had a head like my own. I have been
drunk twice and on each occasion I was made drunk by stupid
people. If I take two drinks I must be in the company of my
closest friends. My limit is generally one, and I take that but
rarely. I can hear the voices of numbers of people who revered
and loved my mother: "Come on, Luce, and 'ave a drink, it'll do
yer good." The usual reply was, "No thanks, another time."
The few times she went for an evening in the pub we detested.
She was never unpleasant, but she was just not our real mother
when she had had two or three half-pints. Our fear, I think, was
that the fullness of her burden might come upon her when she
was not quite herself and like many another she would take her
life. We hated it and we would wait for her and keep close to her
until she was safely asleep.

The power of women to keep the home going and to keep it
together was miraculous, and most mothers did that. It is a
commonplace that people who drink little on an empty stomach
are ill as well as drunk in a very short time, and few Poplar women
at that time had enough to eat. If their burdens were heavy and
they felt their responsibilities, then remorse hit them hard. With
heads afire it was easy to make an end of life. All children were
instinctively fearful when mother had too much to drink. Yet I
must emphasise that it was little that good mothers drank.

My mind began to dwell on the idea of an early marriage to
the queen of my heart. I should doubtless have lived in poverty
of the worst kind, but I am quite sure that it was only the reality
of my calling and the influence of my priest friend and guardian
that kept me from marriage. What a blessing, though, for the girl
in question. She married a man in a good post and with him she
has seen the world and enjoyed a good standard of living. But I
loved sincerely and it was a sweet affection. The height of my
devotion was reached when, longing to see her and hoping that
she might come out for an errand, I looked through the keyhole
of her front door in Suffolk Street. I had my reward, for there she
sat before the fire combing her lovely tresses. Had I been a poet at

fourteen I should have expressed my rapture in verse. Framed in a keyhole, through a slum door, a very young, so very young maiden fair, sat before a fire drawing a comb through her long naturally wavy hair. She might have been singing, for she swayed to and fro. As I watched her for one, two, possibly three minutes, my thoughts were entirely good, inspired by a thing of beauty. That picture has lived with me alone for over fifty years until this minute, and I have loved it. She was my first love.

At the time, I thought that Father Lambert was cruel to try to stop me from forming a steady attachment. Looking back, I can see how wise he was, and how much I owe to his guidance.

What he saw in me I do not know. I was awkward and clumsy, and I did so want to help a lot. I was a bad server at the altar. It took me ages to learn the preparation, and often a candle would not light or would go out after I lit it. It never seemed to happen to others but it happened to me. When little things like that went wrong I got more fussed and then I couldn't think at all.

Remembering these things about myself has made me try to keep my servers comfortable at the altar, by being really patient and kind to them, though I have had my days.

It was wonderful coming into the family of the Lamberts. Perhaps I pushed a bit. I adored Mrs. Lambert; she was so quiet and kind. Their three children were very young. Gladys was a delightful child and one of the things that stands out in my memory is of this little girl of six or seven coming to me, a tough and unattractive lad, to kiss me good night. She had long dark hair, a beautiful oval face with a sweet, happy expression. We were to be as close as brother and sister, though if anything more affectionate, for nearly forty years. The end was tragic, for a "doodle bug" dropped on Father Lambert's vicarage at Norwood and killed Gladys; Father Lambert and his wife were taken to hospital. Father Lambert sent for me. I arrived at the vicarage on a Monday morning. It was just terrible; men were taking for store anything worth salvaging. As I came away from the scene a soldier walked with me to the bus. He was carrying a heavy suitcase. I had no ears for anything much, but I remember him saying, "I have been helping all I could." He had indeed, for had I looked I should have seen that the case he carried had Father Lambert's initials on it and inside that case were intimate treasures of silver and gold. I wonder if that young man ever thought or thinks that he was robbing the dead and the injured.

In Hillingdon Hospital I found a poor broken wreck of a man, crying like a baby. He knew that Gladys had been killed, he had heard her death cries as she was broken to pieces. They had been standing together looking out into the garden when the terrible thing swept down on the house. I got my orders to bury Gladys. On my way back to Norwood Green to find what had happened to the mutilated body I was asked by a police officer if I could identify her. There, among a great number of other bits and pieces of humanity, I looked at the side of a face, and had I failed to recognise the dear features I could never have mistaken her hair. I just knew her. I arranged the funeral.

Returning to the church of St. Mary the Virgin, I found the blast had destroyed the windows and the church was in a bad state. I took off my Army dress jacket and Sam Browne, found a broom and swept the church. Towards the end I was tired and I rested on the broom by the gutter. A car drew up and a big figure in gaiters jumped out. In a heavy demanding tone he asked, "Who are you?" And in a much more demanding tone I said, "Who are you?" He said, "I am the Archdeacon and I am in charge here." I said, "Right, you had better take this broom and finish clearing up while I prepare to receive the body of Father Lambert's daughter." He shook his head, walked to the car slowly and went without a word.

I received Gladys's remains into church a day or two later. We had Vespers. A vigil was kept, I was the watch; alone I watched and prayed through the night in absolute darkness. It was a strange night, and Gladys was particularly near me. It was peaceful and undisturbed, save for the V.1's. They travelled overhead with a light on their tails; some crashed near, some more distantly, but the crash meant death, sorrow and suffering. I was to say something at tomorrow's service about Gladys, and here, kneeling by her coffin, it was easy to prepare, except that I could not see to make a few notes. I said a requiem at 7 a.m. The church was full for the funeral service. After giving dinner, in a British Restaurant to nine East End women who had known and loved Gladys through the years, I made my report to Father Lambert. I gave him every detail, including the words I had spoken. His gratitude was shown by his tears and deep sobbing. Just how I got through those days was something of a mystery to me for I hadn't had a wink of sleep, yet I went through it all calmly and efficiently.

Father Lambert's second child, Doris, was quite different from Gladys. I often thought she should have been a boy, for her grace was that of a tomboy and she would hit as hard. My first recollection of Bernard, the youngest, was when, as a toddler, he first appeared in St. Saviour's School Hall.

With shame covering me now, I recall how I would hang around Father Lambert when he was taking his family out for the day. Quite rightly, he would sometimes just say good-bye and I would nearly choke with disappointment. More often than not, I was invited to join them and I grabbed at the chance selfishly. I learnt to eat and drink without making a noise about it, although it was difficult to keep my mouth closed when I ate, and to drink my soup without supping it up noisily. I know little of English now; I knew nothing then, but I learnt to talk decently and the "was you" gradually disappeared. It was very many years before I could sit down and read a book.

Father Lambert introduced me to the joy of the theatre; good acting gripped me. The story and the theme of the play has never mattered to me much at all. I loved good acting; Matheson Lang and Gladys Cooper in their early days were to me just wonderful. Although I had a good voice and did a great deal of singing I preferred drama, and the heavier the better.

Before Father Lambert came to Poplar, just one entertainment stands out and that was a silent movie. It was called "Our Navy", and I think it must have been a recruiting film. While sailors did all sorts of drills and had lots of fun a great voice gave orders and commented from behind the great white sheet. I remember thinking how wonderful the Navy was.

Before 1914 I hardly ever had more than sixpence a week out of the little money I earned, so if Father Lambert hadn't allowed me to go to "The Glen", Southend, for a holiday, I should not have left Poplar at all. Even so, I earned my keep, for I would saw wood for the fires by the hour and single-handed. After sawing and chopping to the right length and thickness, then stacking tidily in the store, I enjoyed the feeling of satisfaction and the look of gratitude from my good guardian.

At "The Glen" our fun was simple and tough. We walked and sang, we swam and we ate. Night bathes were a special feature. The stretch of Southend mud made it impossible to bathe when the tide was low, but when it was high tide at night there was nothing more lovely than swimming out into black darkness. I felt I could swim for years, for ever, and never tire. As for walking, a great line of us, mostly boys, but sometimes girls too, would swing along from Southend to Westcliff and back to "The Glen", just singing our hearts out all the way. It was grand. We always had people interested and amused.

What wasn't so lovely was going back to London. For me it meant a very empty pocket, and Mother felt the pinch too, because she would somehow have to feed me for a week and wait till Saturday for the meagre ten or twelve shillings I earned, for we were not paid for holidays. Poor Mother never had a holiday for many years to come.

CHAPTER VI

The War

SOON after the war began, in 1914, I joined the Army, and this was probably the most important thing that ever happened to me. It took me away from Poplar, away from my own class, and taught me to mix with all sorts of people on the same level.

I joined the 4th Essex Regiment and we were sent to defend the shores of England. Our assignment was Yarmouth. We made trenches on the sands and we made sand-pies, and in our idle moments we put wasps in spiders' webs.

We kept watch out to sea from the pier. On Britannia Pier our eyes were often towards the land with our backs to the enemy. This happened every morning when the girls, without shame or in complete ignorance of our presence, would undress, bathe and dry themselves under our very eyes.

While in Yarmouth my soccer prowess was brought into play and I might have been in the battalion XI but for a kick in the knee which laid me up for nearly two months. That was a deadly dull period for it was late spring and I could not leave my billet.

I had never tasted independence before going into the Army. Now I had 3s. 6d. a week to play with, after allotting my mother 8s. I thought Army life was wonderful. The exercises in the open air made me strong. We marched for miles with our heavy loads, and we sang as we marched. The food was poor and it had a sameness, but it was enough. Further, my uniform was the same as everybody else's. Smartness and cleanliness counted, and I was smart and clean.

Because of this I was able to get into a decent set among the privates, and learnt how to enjoy good society. Two special friends,

Oxborough and Ross, did a lot for me. They were well-mannered, well-educated, good types. Unlike me, neither of them went to church regularly. Both were older than I. Oxo had a delightful girl to whom he was engaged and was terrified of losing her. George was specially good-looking, tall with a twinkle in his eye.

George led me into the most delightful temptations, for he opened the way for me into the society of girls. I knew little about them, in spite of my overcrowded existence in Poplar, and apart from the strangeness of my growing body had no understanding whatever of the relationship of men and women. I remember being horrified at the age of about fourteen when an older lad poured into my ear all he knew about sex. My ideas being vague, I was terrified of anything beyond a brief stolen kiss. Well, George and I met two girls; he made his choice and I took the other. Until that time I had regarded the opposite sex as gracious and wonderful and any prying into their attractions gave me a sense of shame. Here, however, was a revelation. This lady was puzzled, for I could not be seduced.

Soon after this experience I was roller skating on Wellington Pier. There was little I could not do on skates. I was happy to enjoy the fun alone but was always ready to give a helping hand. A little boy kept falling down and cracking his knees as he tried to master the art, so I picked him up and took him round the rink once or twice. This gave him confidence and put him on the right track. For that I was thanked by the boy, Eric Hinde, and by his sister, Marion, then about the age of sixteen years. From that time until now we have remained the very closest of friends. Here was a landmark indeed in my progress in social experience.

My interest in acquiring good manners and easy speech kept me quiet in the company of people who enjoyed homes and education of a superior kind. But I could talk to Marion and Eric and a younger Hinde still, Peggy, and I loved their company. They were on holiday in Yarmouth, having come from Norwich. When they went home it was not long before I received an invitation for a week-end. Theirs was the largest private house I had ever been in and it had a lovely big garden. I talked freely only when I was with Marion and the other youngsters, but that place was heaven to me and I was anxious not to put a foot wrong, lest the link be broken.

I adored Marion, because she was so kind and good. With very good reason, Frank Hinde, her father, didn't encourage me, though he was happy to entertain a soldier. I did write "thank you" letters, but he must have found them poor stuff, if indeed he could read them at all. It was good to see Mr. and Mrs. Hinde after my ordination and to tell them what their kind hospitality meant to me in those days.

It is well over forty-five years now since I first met Marion and our friendship has been a most wonderful treasure. We have compared notes and helped each other very many times. In those early days her calm cultured mind and most charitable outlook helped and steadied me, and her friendship was a very important part of my education. And through the years she has continued to influence me for good. Many others would say the same about her. She could have gone far in the field of education had she been given the opportunity, but like all fathers of standing in those days, her father thought higher education was for boys; the girls didn't matter so much. As things have worked out, her life has been difficult but splendidly helpful. She has borne with courage a great load of trouble of her own, and she helps with the problems and cares of numbers of young people who wisely turn to her in their need.

She married a doctor who died tragically. He left two sons, Hugh and John, and she has kept a home going for them, and for many others in need of love and care. Her bounty and kindliness have drawn relatives and friends to her. Her letters to me, during the First World War and since, I have kept and treasured. Beautifully written, models of sense and wisdom, they are full of good cheer. Always she makes little of her own problems and views the future hopefully. Marion Mackie made her mark, and a lasting one, on my life.

When I was ordained, she gave me a small Prayer Book. She wrote in the front page:

> The Glory of life is to love
> Not to be loved
> To give not to get
> To serve not to be served

To be a strong hand in the dark
To another in a time of need
To be a cup of strength
To any soul in a crisis of weakness
This is to know the glory of life.

From Yarmouth I moved to Thetford where it was really tough going. We were miles from the town, and under canvas. While I was there I learned to gamble for money on pontoon and brag, but losing my 3s. 6d. within an hour of being paid seemed to me poor fun, so I packed it up.

We seemed to spend most of our time drilling, and I saw so many men with fallen arches and galled feet from their ill-fitting boots that I became terribly afraid of losing my own foot arches. I used to do exercises on my toes to keep the spring and resilience of my feet.

There was one particular officer named Haylock who used to drill us for hours. He seemed to love the sound of his own voice, and the echo of his "A-bout turn" or "Slo-ope arms. Inter-file. Right turn," with the well-tuned and incessant "Left right, left right, left right," and "Form fours," then for a change, "Form two deep," and "Right incline." Then, feeling generous, "Halt," he would spit at us, and "Ri'dress," then "Order arms. Stand at ease.—Shun."

So often we were nearly rested and set going again. We were being made into the best company and it was hell.

It was while this kind of training was going on that I tried my hand, or my voice rather, at ventriloquism. I could mimic the Adjutant perfectly in his words of command and his calling of officers. He didn't like Mr. Haylock very much and often he tore out the word "Haylock" as if he were addressing a drunk being prepared for the Commanding Officer. It was with all this venom, while we were marching in line by the right, 100 yards or more away from the officer, that I shouted in perfect Adjutant fashion, "Haylock." That officer was still singing out "Lef'ri', lef'ri' " as a sort of warning that he was about to order, "About turn," for we were marching away from his standing still position. The command "Halt" came across the air, followed quickly by "About turn.

Stand at ease." Then we watched our Mr. Haylock go to the
Battalion H.Q. and a little later return.

My effort was not altogether appreciated by the other men.
Although some were amused most of them blinded and cursed me
for a fool, for he had left us not "Easy" but "At ease," which was
almost as trying as being left at the "Slope" position.

Whatever happened in the Orderly Room, we were dismissed
very soon afterwards. I visualised my efficient officer going to the
Adjutant and smartly saluting and awaiting orders. The much
more efficient and very superior Adjutant, I saw raising an eye-
brow and saying. "What the hell do you want?" Poor Haylock
would stammer and retire and both would think the other mad.
The practical joke came off, but I think a little bird squeaked.

Soon after this the Company was taken on a forced march with
full kit. Feeling ran very high as we went on and on at attention
with never a suggestion of "changing arms" or "marching at ease."
At last I revolted and called the sergeant to ask the officer to be
allowed to "change arms" as my left arm had cramp. Nothing happened and I changed arms. I was for it when I returned, and Haylock said I would be court martialled. The thought of the "glass-
house" put the fear of the devil into me. I had every kind of Act
read to me.

When I got free that evening I sorted out the Padre—Barry, now
Bishop of Southwell—and told him all about it. Just why I am so
certain it was Barry is because I spoke to only two padres in the
Army during the years 1914-18. The other one I hunted for just
before I went up the line. When I found him I had to teach him how
to hear my confession; he hadn't a clue. I can see his silly,
fat, pompous form standing before me. He stood all the time and
I kept him standing, a long time for I made a full and careful
confession.

I got out of my trouble, through Padre Barry, I think, and I got
three days confined to barracks. I thought C.B. was easy until then.
Every half-hour the bugle sounded "You can be a defaulter as long
as you like, so long as you answer your name." Directly that call
sounded you had to run to the Guardroom where the Orderly
Sergeant called the roll. Nobody knows more than a defaulter how

soon half an hour can pass away. When it was wet and cold it seemed that you were no sooner out of your tunic and pack than you were in it again at the double. Ten times you would answer that call from 5 p.m. until 10 p.m. Often you had dirty fatigues to do between times, but you had to be clean at roll-call.

I missed going to the Dardanelles by a very narrow margin. I had "water on the knee"; the joint was stiff and fat and felt numb, yet it was painful, for weeks. I was sorry at the time, but not so sorry later, for the County Regiments of the Norfolks and Essex were reduced to a skeleton of their original strength.

While unfit for parades I served as a batman. My allotted officer was a first lieutenant, named Strong. He was quiet and efficient but he was never conversational with me. I was there to clean his room, polish his boots and buttons, brush his clothes, prepare his bath, light his fire, do whatever he told me to do. He gave me my half-crown a week and I was glad of it. Our relationship was that of master and man of the time, 1915—I was a chattel. He felt nothing amiss in not saying "Good morning" or anything else except, "Williamson, my Sam Browne," "Williamson, my boots," "Williamson, my bath," or, on Friday nights, "There's your half-crown"; which, fitting to our relationship, was put on the table and never handed to me. I picked it up.

I have sometimes wondered what happened to him. He was the type who would fight and die bravely. He would care for his men, dare and die for them, but he just wouldn't want to know them. Had I gone with him to the front line as his batman he would never have said anything, I think, but "Williamson, my dinner," "Williamson, my sleeping bag," "Williamson, go away." Such treatment was no hardship to me, however, and I felt no bitterness. Social grading of that kind seemed natural, whether due to money, breeding, education, or just luck; some were up and the others down.

What I did resent was the upstart and the temporary officer who was never really fit to command; the man who showed off and made himself offensive by trying to be superior. This sort of showing off occurred when an old friend, formerly a private, turned up to see Father Lambert at Poplar. George was a six-footer, resplendent in his new officer's uniform. Father Lambert was very glad to see him, for when George and I and two others were in Yarmouth, the good Father came from London for a few days and gave us all a very good time. Before George sat down, Father said, "What luck, Joe is coming on leave today, we can all go out to a show together like old times." Poor George felt the weight of his single pip and said, "I am sorry, I can't go out with Joe as I am an officer now." Without a word, he was shown to the door and bade farewell. There were officers and officers and it was sad to see some good uniforms spoilt by the stupid, stuck-up bodies inside them.

Having missed going to the Dardanelles with the 4th Essex, I was sent to France when I was fit to join the 11th Royal Fusiliers.

After a few weeks of intense training we were sent "up the line" without an idea as to what we should do, how far we should go, or what territory we should be covering. The one thing of which we were sure was that we were going "over the top" soon after we arrived in the front line. So far as I was concerned—and I think it was the same with all the men—it was a case of going up and over blindfold, I didn't know a thing.

We started marching towards the front line after dinner, and we never stopped until we got there at about 10 o'clock, in pitch darkness. One effort had been made to give us refreshment on the way— a petrol can full of tea was passed from one to the other as we stumbled on. I got a mouthful of tea-leaves, but they were moist and I held on to them and drew the taste of tea from them. I handed the tin back to the next man and hurried on to keep contact.

At the front line the lights from the German lines swept over us and hovered for many minutes like fierce and efficient street lamps until we felt naked of shelter or protection. We soon learnt that to keep still gave us a chance of remaining unobserved, no matter how bright the lights, and that if we moved it meant almost certain death by machine-gun fire or sniping. On that first night in the trenches, our officers and N.C.O's were so ill-informed that we were at first posted the wrong way round. It was not their fault, and the error was soon corrected. The fact was that Rejoiner Trench was

F

no trench at all, it was like a series of massive shell-holes. The back and front were much the same.

It was very late when we were in position. The awful atmosphere, as well as the mud, glued me to the spot where I stood. Machine-guns were busy and whizz-bangs came over, noisy enough to split your ear-drums. The floating lights were uncanny as they sat in the air to show up every moving thing, yet mercifully never to reveal animate objects if they stayed still. What nerve soldiers had to have looking into no-man's-land! Their eyes dare not blink in the face of those glaring lights. It felt, of course, as if everybody in the world was looking at you and that any second a bullet would go through your face. Too often it did, for both Germans and Allied soldiers were very brave and could be but a few yards away, and sentries on the firestep were sitting targets.

I took my turn at first looking into no-man's-land. It was grey-black—they call it dawn. Every movement of a rustling or a waving of long grass tore the eyes out of my head with looking. A rat the size of a good big kitten moved across my front a few feet away. Surely it was somebody crawling towards me. I didn't speak, nor did my companion; everything was deadly quiet except for a very distant melancholy rat-tat-tat of a machine-gun. Then the bushes came to shape themselves in the growing light. My eyes didn't roam, though. I kept them locked and steady to my front. The men in the trench standing to depended on me. We were called down and another two put up while, and only while, we had our rum ration. What rum! It took a long time to get down, it was hot and truly burning and it took my breath away and made my weak head sing. Up again. And then came an appalling crack, it shook me through and set my legs out of control. Surely I couldn't live through this, something must hit me. With the man beside me I popped up and down with shells dropping all round and machine-guns hard at it. As I bobbed down I saw the men lying in the bottom of the trench with their heads almost buried. One head was up. It was the Sergeant's. He looked at me and shouted, "Up, up." It was an hour of agony for anyone on the firestep and no man could ever get used to that. It shook me in every nerve. When I was relieved I sank into the bottom of the trench. I hadn't collapsed, I was just like the others, bowed, lying with my head in the clay; eyes closed, I saw pictures of home.

The bombardment went on for six hours. We thought Jerry was coming over, Jerry thought we were; neither moved and the shelling thinned out.

My first day in the front line was a very horrible one, it rained and rained. We slid about the trench and its communications, our rifles got jammed up, we had no bread. We ate soft cheese and drank water.

A frightful shock came to us all, we were to go over the top the next morning. Freshers like myself didn't know what we were in for but the rest did. There wasn't a smile among us except the smile of despair. Going over to attack in this mud meant murder, you couldn't move. After scrambling to the top the men would stand knee deep in clay, soft clay like quicksand. They would stick there until a bullet found them.

The late evening brought no change in orders or the weather.

I stood for an hour on the firestep with a man who was badly shell-shocked. We had bare knees. This poor man could not control his legs nor his head. His knees literally crashed against each other, the dull thuds hurt those of us who heard them. He tried so hard to control himself he would strain at his head and then, like a jack-in-the-box, his head would jerk up and down. He was carried away with his knees like balloons and his head swinging.

I lasted that night only in my first venture in the front line. It went on raining through the night. Our holes in the wall took our soaking bodies. I must have fallen asleep and until "Stand to" I was as one dead. I fell out of my hole, but I was tied up from my head down to my toes with cramp. I could not shake it off. My neck was solid, all my muscles were lumps of torture. How I tried to get free! If you could crawl it was better than going on a stretcher. It was so hard on the men who tried to carry you knee deep in mud, slipping and falling.

So I started for our dressing station and was given a direction. After being examined by a doctor, I was again directed to the road to Albert, on which road our headquarters was stationed. As I staggered and crawled I got the full blast of hidden batteries; one gun was so near me that my right ear began to sing after the blast and has never ceased since. The ear was operated on after the war and the drum taken away, I think, for the cavity is very large and the hearing is nil; it still sings, though.

Just near that gun, horses were trying to pull another gun out and bit by bit the horses sank in the dreadful mud. I pressed on in pain and spared myself the horror of seeing the horses shot just before they disappeared, beaten by mud and water.

It seemed many hours before I reached our base headquarters and I haven't an idea how I found it. When I did, there was a great open fire going, with a big cauldron of bully beef stew, steaming hot. The heat of the fire seemed to draw me and as I felt the heat I fell in absolute agony; I was exhausted and hungry, as well as being gripped with cramp. The cooks were good to me, I was given dry clothes and fed, but to the casualty clearing station I had to go and I was put to bed before being shifted to a base hospital. After a few days I was up and helping sisters and nurses to make beds. That was more than nice, for a very young Sister Steel—the name sticks— was especially kind. Together we were very good at bed-making, but very much better at it after our heads had met while tucking in the bottom part of a bed. How time flies! She would be about sixty-five or sixty-six as I record our bit of fun. She was kind, but then sisters and nurses are cunning. Sister Steel wanted someone to shave wounded men; men who couldn't help themselves. With patience and care I shaved men for the first time. How patient they had to be with me, and some of them were very sore after the operation; still they were grateful and Sister allowed me to help her with bed-making and bed-changing. Just by the way, there were a few bed-pans and bottles to deal with too.

I was back at the Infantry Base Depot at Etaples in no time, it seemed. We were under canvas in that vast camp of sand. Barbed wire yards high formed our bounds. It was there that I met "Sully", John Sullivan, a young Roman Catholic, a tough lad. He liked to go to his Mass and I liked to go to mine. Before I met him I was put in a tent which was already very full before I was added to the number. The men had had a pay day and were together in the wet canteen.

I made my narrow bed with my one blanket on the top of my groundsheet, my trousers and tunic folded made my pillow. My greatcoat went on top. I felt lonely and sad but in the darkness I said my prayers, kneeling in my long pants, socks and shirt, before I wriggled myself down my tube of a blanket. I might have got to sleep but just didn't make it before bugles sounded, canteens stopped selling and singing soldiers made their way to their tents. My tent companions were all really drunk and came in singing and stinking; not all, but some were sick at once. Without a word I found my trousers and greatcoat and went out. I knelt in the depth of a sand-dune. The night was lovely but cold. I prayed. I might have wished I could drink and get drunk too, for to be the only sober man in a crowded tent wasn't nice. Out on the sand the singing, the cursing, the fighting for miles around got less and less. Then all was still and peaceful. I crept back to my tent. The atmosphere was thick and evil-smelling but I was tired. I struck a match and saw a place I could sit without being faced by a drunken man. God was kind. I might have stayed awake listening to the rattles, the snores, the whistles, a chorus indeed, not two alike, but I put my tired body down and sleep claimed me.

During the training at Etaples I cut my thumb badly. I wear the two inch scar now. It took a long time to heal and that was how I met the two youngsters, Sully and Fred. Poor Fred. He was eighteen and had been up the line in an Infantry unit and had nearly gone mad. He had seen a red-haired woman running along the parapet, and that was that. Night—all night—and day she haunted him. How Sully and I tried to get him right, but his red-haired woman ate him up. Sully was game and sane. We walked and talked and thought about God, yet we were tough and crude. We were not morbid. We were not sentimental. We were happy and natural and we talked about God. We had something to hope for.

A Miss Pattinson, of East Harling, Norfolk, had a friend who had been badly wounded and died in hospital at Etaples and was buried there. Could I find his grave? It took us a whole day, but here it was, his name, number and everything. By that grave, Sully, a Roman Catholic, and I, an Anglican, solemnly knelt, solemnly crossed ourselves, solemnly prayed for his soul. When I said, "Rest eternal grant unto him, O Lord, and let light perpetual shine upon him, may he have peace," Sully said, "It's funny, we say the same prayers."

I don't think I was a bit in advance of him regarding education and general knowledge. I was older by two or three years and I was a little more free of speech. Together we were very close to the earth. We had no money and somehow we didn't worry about that. We were happy to walk and to talk. The quoting of the Hail Mary, my repetition of the Catholic—not Roman Catholic—prayers of Faith, Hope and Love, my habit of confession—that in the Church of England was more than he could understand. We were too ignorant to argue but we weren't too ignorant to feel and to know we were akin in faith and worship. Our friendship was absolutely clean, we didn't want to talk of things questionable or cheap. We slept together for warmth, we were closer than brothers. We knelt in silence by our bed before we turned in. We fought once, and it was a bitter fight; it was lovely, though, to be able to wash ourselves, go for a long walk and forget all about it.

Extraordinary though it may seem, I remember nothing of our parting and I have nothing to guess at nor do I remember how long we were together at Etaples. The bulk of my four years in the Army is forgotten. The things I remember are the pickings, the bright and the dark things.

On my way up the line again I was near Arras. A bunch of us were together, no one knowing anybody else. As was the custom, we gradually got together and we listened to each other. The conversation was on the curse of being away from home and away from the girls. Out came the usual smart and smutty stories, we ate them up and one outdid the other. I hadn't joined in, but only because my memory was bad; I couldn't store stories of legs and arms and sexual intercourse. Anyhow, one did bubble up into my mind and it seemed about time for the limelight to flash on me. The eyes and ears came my way and out my story came. The story I don't remember, but I remember a face and a pair of eyes looking into my very soul and draining the blood from my head. The man was a private soldier of about twenty-six or seven. His face was handsome and strong, his dark eyes never flinched, they held my own and I could not take my eyes away. My story was told to him, at him, and it lost its point. My voice went on without feeling or interest. I was glad when it was over. I walked away to be alone. I felt terribly ashamed. Then I found I wasn't alone and the voice of the man who had looked at me said, "I am surprised at you." No more than that. I had no more conversation with him and I don't remember seeing him again. Why did he pick on me? Why didn't he interfere with the others? I couldn't understand it and I still don't understand it, but it happened.

I still have a fairly good voice but before and during the war I had a grand voice, and nothing gave me greater joy than to get away from everybody and sing my heart out. I knew every line of Gounod's Mass and no part did I like better than the Sanctus solos, and I would fling them across fields, old trenches and the open spaces. Often I would think I was mad, but I was one of the few sane ones, really, and knew a peace of heart rare among men at that time and in that place.

While I was in Yarmouth a concert party pianist had given me a song called "Absent". It was very full of sentiment, all about "long shadows on the grass" and "thinking I hear thee call". He taught me to sing it and I treasured it. It was always in my pack. The difficulty was to get somebody to play and, of course, a piano to play on.

On my way back to my unit, without an idea as to how I should get to it, I was ordered to a casualty clearance station to unload stores. There were German prisoners working there. After two hours' work we had tea in a hall with a stage and there, sure enough, was a piano. One fellow began to hammer out a tune with one finger. A tall, distinguished looking German cast longing eyes on the piano. I spotted his interest and made signs. He smiled, looked about the hall for his escort and then came to the piano. He struck a chord but then exercised his fingers and rubbed them, shaking his head pathetically. Then he played and it was a joy to watch him with his eyes closed and to listen to his music. Soon I had my song out and he accompanied me beautifully. It was great fun until the corporal escort missed the prisoner. I took the blame and the corporal was kind. While we were at the piano the war was forgotten, I wanted his playing, he liked my voice and the men around enjoyed the respite from war.

It was at this place that I was first introduced to a French brothel. Like most young men I was laughed into it, though perhaps "sneered into it" is the best translation of the mood. "You're afraid," they laughed. "I don't believe 'e's ever 'ad a woman," said an older man. "Come on, it'll do yer good, it's only five francs." It was cold in this dreadful cobbled floor room, with the windows all blown out, and when those men had gone there was nothing but black night and loneliness for me. So I went, scared stiff, like a lamb to the slaughter or to the shearing. How well I remember thinking how clean East London was compared with this. The other five men kept up a mad conversation with roars of laughter as they tried to work themselves up to the excitement of the "Red Lamp" where it was all fun. My poor weak brain was wondering if in fact these men had been in as many brothels and had as many women as they said. Further, I wondered if some of them were just being brave in talk because they were faint in heart. They knew the drill of every "Red Lamp". A government doctor examined the women once a week, it was on Monday mornings. There was no chance at all of getting a dose. It took little calculation to weigh up the chances of disease if the doctor did examine the women once a week. Men flocked in night after night, not only our men but many nationalities besides, as well as Frenchmen. If the women were clean many men weren't and so there was always a stream of men going down to the Base to hospital. We all knew, or thought we knew, that one of our biggest hospitals at Rouen was full of men who had venereal disease. It was said that they had their money stopped while they were ill.

So we drew near through a dismal alley to the brothel. The woman on the door was old and ugly. She squealed out her piece, in the middle of which was "jig-a-jig". Bravely the rest marched in laughing and shouting. I followed, not half so bravely and very quiet. It was cold and cheerless outside but inside the overheated foul air nearly sent my head reeling. That, with dreadful cracked music being blasted out of an instrument, plus everybody talking and laughing and some singing against the music was the sum total of sound and density. Of course, there was a bar, and whatever it was that counted as beverage put you in merry if not stupid heart in express time.

All round the room and on the ceiling were mirrors, so that whichever way you looked you saw women, up to middle age. I should rather say parts of women; bare arms, bare legs and everything else, for there seemed to be dozens of women and all they had on was a fancy frock to the thigh and from the bosom. Many of them were mixed up with men, nobody was hidden in this great, hot room crowded with solid seats.

We sat down and I was glad to sit down or I think I should have fallen. But no sooner had I sat down than a great, fat thing sat on my knee and smothered me with herself. She was painted and powdered; she sweated through it all. In my struggle to be free of her I felt thoroughly outraged and furious. She sensed this and tried to be gentle and that was worse. It was like being caught up by an octopus. It ended by me getting my face smacked but somehow the laugh was on her and not on me. She left me but the others had their arms full and very soon three of them were trailing after their conquerors. There was a desk at which they paid their money and the women picked up little buckers which had brushes in them. I longed to get out into the cold air but I was afraid of losing my way so I waited with the two men who had made excuses for not going upstairs and had infuriated their partners.

Altogether it was a dirty business in a horrible atmosphere. Only war, aimlessness and having nothing to do could send droves of our men into places like that. Hot air, drink and the devil got most men, although some went coldly and deliberately. It couldn't attract me. We talked as we went along. It was jocular in a quiet sort of way. We talked of the horrible lives of the prostitutes and I remember being brave enough to say that they were somebody's sisters.

I was no sooner in the line than I was out again, or so it seemed; without the aid of bullets or shells. The cold and the wet got at me and stiffened me. I can't think I was really weak, yet I was back in

England, and my category lowered in the matter of about two months. I had a toe off, I was deaf, or nearly deaf in my right ear, which made it sing and often hurt and there was a discharge. My eyes had got really bad and I realised I had about half the sight of one eye only, my left one was useless. Yet after I left Hammersmith General Hospital I was wonderfully fit. The men who were in the infantry and were in the trenches over and over again and came out of it fit were super-men; there were not many of them.

From hospital I went to the Duke of York's School, Dover. Night after night we went into the tunnels while German aircraft were overhead. One lovely summer day I sat and watched the first daylight raid on Folkestone. Many German aircraft took part. They were no height at all and from every kind of naval craft sitting in Dover Harbour guns were firing, yet the planes went on serenely and seemingly undisturbed.

Later I saw a daylight raid on London. It was on a Saturday morning. I was on leave and Father Lambert had an outing for the Sunday School children to Epping Forest. Very low indeed came thirty or forty and perhaps more, loud and daring German aircraft. We had nothing to hit them with and no aircraft with which to match them. Literally, they seemed to take their time to do their bombing and go back home. It seemed shocking to me. What was even more shocking was that the train load of children was left by the driver and fireman and guard. They went to a tunnel and I was left with another lad and Father Lambert to see the children out of the carriages into the tunnel. The aircraft were just above us when the last of the children gained the tunnel. Afterwards we got back into the train and completed our day's outing. Among other damage a convent school in Commercial Road was hit during this raid, and children were killed.

My category was lowered and I was then detailed to serve as batman to a Captain Ford who was chosen to go on to a Senior Officers' course at Aldershot.

A bad memory of that course was the drunken fury of a giant brother batman. He had slipped away to his wife for a week-end, and had asked me to cover his absence by doing his work. I said I would try but, of course, it went wrong. I cleaned the officer's Sam Browne and boots, and carefully laid out his clothes for dinner. I managed to dodge in and out without being seen until the man was called for personally. I asked if I could do anything. Where was Evans? "I will try and find him, sir." I pretended to look and went back in the hope that he would give me something to do. Not a bit of it, Evans had done it before and I was told to go to hell. No matter what time he returned I was ordered to tell Evans to report to his officer. When Evans did turn up he was half drunk. He came straight to me by my bed and asked if all was well. I had to tell him, and off he went to a not very good-tempered officer anyhow. He came back fuming and I tried to keep as quiet and understanding as all the men were. I had gone to bed. Soon I was to be as close to death as is possible. He let out foul curses at me for telling his "something" officer where he was, and he put his bayonet on his rifle, which nobody saw in the semi-darkness. The next thing I knew was the big furious man above me with the bayonet pointing down at me. There must have been a terrific change in my appearance which made him realise what he was about to do. I could not speak but he paused and then went away with his rifle. Nobody spoke, nor did anybody mention it the next day. I often wondered if he felt the hangman's rope round his neck or saw in my eyes the glassy look of a dead man.

It must have been towards the end of 1917 when I was sent to a Labour Unit and was stationed at Beddington in Surrey. The countryside was very lovely, set off by a most beautiful old church amidst spacious grounds and grand trees. Some of the old houses had become derelict, the grounds had been neglected, others were pretty well ruins or made so by Army occupation.

Having a voice, I was put in a concert party. Some of the artists were old professionals. One of them had been with a fair and was an acrobat. We were a mixed crowd but on the whole a very happy one. We filled the Queen's Hall, Croydon, and travelled around a good bit. Our Army life was made up of fatigues and rehearsals.

At Beddington I was introduced into a most outstanding and lovely family. There were three middle-aged sisters. Two of them,

Shade and Katie Harding, were service companions to Miss Collyer Bristow, a very gracious, aristocratic old lady. Another sister, Alice, was married to a schoolmaster, Charles Dean. All of them lived at a lovely old house called Beddington Cottage, but the Deans and the two sisters had two nice adjoining houses in Waddon Road, Croydon, which were let to friends.

The Hardings and the Deans were the kindest and most peaceful people I have ever met. They always made excuses for other people and never spoke badly of anyone. They called me "Cheerio", and welcomed me into their home. As I write Shade is still alive and is over ninety.

The atmosphere of Beddington Cottage made me think once more of my own call to the priesthood, still very much a personal, secretive thing. I had developed a very great deal and my outlook had broadened, but although I could talk more freely, I was still very ignorant. My reading, writing and spelling were very, very poor; my reading was very slow and my writing still very laborious. But here in Charlie Dean and the ladies I had all the sympathy and understanding possible. I told them of my birth, my mother and my closest sister, Clara, who for reasons unknown has always been called Doll. It was not long before I told them of my call. They were deeply interested and saw no reason why it should not be realised. Miss Collyer Bristow was very much the great lady but she was most gracious. I spent a deal of time with her and sang to her many times. I didn't actually mention my vocation to her but Kate Harding did. "Here is where Leonard will help," said Miss Bristow. Leonard was her nephew, Bishop Borrows, Bishop of Sheffield, who had been at one time Vicar of Croydon. Strings were pulled and I was to see the great man on his visit to his aunt. They all thought the world of the Bishop, and hopes of help and guidance for "Cheerio" ran high. The Bishop saw me. He was affable, patronising and loud. What school had I been to? Where did I live? Then, quite shortly, I was put out of his mind as he said, "Learn a trade and go to the mission field as a layman." He almost shook my hand. He pushed his short self outwards because he had no height and stalked away like a fat cockerel. That was that. What he probably never knew was how he dropped in the estimation of the household, including that of his aunt; all were sad and disappointed.

Orders for embarkation came through and we went on leave. All who had any idea about entertainment or could sing or play a musical instrument were to go to the Entertainment Base Depot, Rouen. We actually went to France the day after the Armistice was signed.

It seemed to be stupid going to France when it was all over, as we thought. My first effort as a showman was in the *Théâtre des Arts*, Rouen. From there I was sent to a place near Arras to join a concert party which was to go to Cologne to entertain the Army of Occupation.

I didn't want to go to Cologne and I stated my desire to go back to England to study for Holy Orders. I saw General Ellis of the Tank Corps and he said I must go to the Rhine and assured me that I should only be there for a year. I was told not to be a fool and that now the war was over we should all have a good time, and I should have the best time of all doing nothing but rehearse for shows we should put out.

That future didn't attract me but I knew I should not be freed in spite of Duration of War pledges, so without batting an eyelid I took off my glasses as I left H.Q. and flung them on the ground and broke them. Without sight I was no good to anybody and without my glasses I was just like that. Anything might have happened to me then, but it didn't. Reporting sick, the M.O. did not hesitate to send me back to the Base Hospital. An oculist saw me and he looked to be a good sort. Quite frankly and truthfully I told him my story. Just as frankly he told me he would have to fix me up with new glasses and send me back where I came from. He must have seen my deep disappointment. I became silent and entirely co-operative as he looked at my eyes. The only words we exchanged, apart from my "Thank you," were when I got my glasses about a fortnight later. He then said, "Your eyes are bad." I replied: "Are they?" although I knew they were very bad.

I went back to my marquee ward feeling terribly depressed. Not half an hour later, names were being called for standing sick cases for England. I heard "Private Williamson, Joseph," and for a moment I couldn't reply. Then my name was called again. I answered and hurried forward and the R.A.M.C. Sergeant looked at me and said "Debility."

That was indeed my weakness, for when the oculist told me I must go back to my unit, I just gave up. I was drained of interest and concern and I think I would rather have spent the rest of my days in clink than sing songs and take part in sketches to amuse the Occupation forces.

Before I was boarded, an oculist at the hospital told me he thought he could restore the sight of my left eye if I would allow him to operate. I didn't consent, and although I am still blind in the left eye to the extent of knowing only light and dark, without the power to distinguish people, letters, or numbers, or to see to walk straight, I am glad I did not allow him to meddle. The best oculists have never suggested an operation.

I had a Medical Board and was given a 50 per cent pension, which was about 18s. a week, and my condition was to be reviewed each year. I was discharged with honour and a thank you from the King. I still have my certificate, and it is most beautifully scribed; hundreds of thousands received them.

CHAPTER VII

Training for Ordination

THE world had opened to me with the war. I was homesick for a bit and felt nervous and a little afraid, but after a week my home was the Army and all I needed was on my person and the rest in the barrack room or in the billet. The half-hour parade before breakfast was good. I never got enough to eat but I felt fit and I was fit. To me it was like a long holiday, it was so different from Poplar and and my work and poor pay. Although I only had 3s. 6d. a week it was 2s. 6d. more than I could take from my mother while at home. The social side was good. I was a soldier and soldiers were popular. In Poplar my outlook was always limited and cramped; in the Army a soldier, even a Tommy, was noticed. Then I was often left alone patrolling, alert, on the spot, quick to challenge; it was good for me. As to the war proper, I never gave it a thought until I got near it. Army life was a big life, you travelled and saw places and met people and listened to people. Perhaps most important of all was the discipline; you did what you were told or you suffered. I did what I was told. I broke bounds and was out after lights but I never got drunk and was alert enough to get past a guard or scale a wall. I went into the Army weak and a mere boy. I came out a strong man, except for my eyes and my ear. Though not much improved as to learning, my mind and outlook were bigger, I had taste and some dignity. The Army did me good.

I hadn't the slightest idea how to buy a suit, and my first attempt to select my own clothes was, I knew, a complete failure. For a bit I thought I looked rather good, but the feeling of being conspicuous died on me and I wanted to be the same as most people. In a uniform you may be anybody, you are ironed out, you are all the same or there is at least a sameness. In Civvy Street, you are placed by your taste; if you are showy, you show off, if you are modest, unassuming and reserved, you are one of many. There were times when I had to push, there were many more times when I should have done far better by not pushing. Without turning a hair and not fearing to be brutal, Father Lambert would say, "You are wonderful, Joe, until you open your mouth." I was saved for what I became by being able to take that kind of blunt truth, for truth it was.

It is over forty years ago, but I can feel my position then as if it were today, and in one sense my disability today is the same as it was then. I lacked culture. I had no reading and found it hard to read. I could write very little and the little I did write took me a long time. My English was guided by sound, not by knowledge of the grammar. I still do not know a thing about style. Very little of the knowledge I possessed had been imparted to me through school lessons. Son of my mother, I was made in her image; her natural outlook and actions were and always have been my standard. She could neither read nor write, yet she could calculate, she was rarely done. Nobody had more of the wisdom of God than she, nobody was more selfless. Like her, all that I possessed was in my mind and in my heart. Like her again, I had always been happy in manual labour. All that being so, there was nothing by which to judge myself apart from my simple prayers and worship. All that is absorbed in a general disciplined education, which so greatly influences and steadies an individual, I had none of it.

Am I paying as full a tribute as I ought to Father Lambert? On one of the forms I had to fill in I put him down as my guardian. I cannot gauge what I gained by watching him and listening to him, but perhaps his watching me and listening to me was even more important. Not "was you", but "were you", he would say; "neither nor, either or", and so on. I remember repeating "were you, were you", until he said, "That is just right."

When I came home to my mother in Poplar, I found myself homesick for the Army. "What are you going to do, Joe?" asked

My mother, "one of nature's greatest ladies".

75 Arcadia Street, Poplar, where I was born on June 15th, 1895. Nine of us lived in two upstairs rooms.

We often played by the "Lim'ous Cut". There was no protecting wall in those days, and suicides by drowning were common.

Joining the Army was probably the most important thing that happened to me.

My first job, at 14, was as a page boy at Radlett.

After I was ordained, I used to help Father Lambert in his summer camps, to pay him back for having stolen his change as a boy.

My family have always
been the greatest help
to me, and now they
are grown up, with
children of their own,
we are closer than ever.

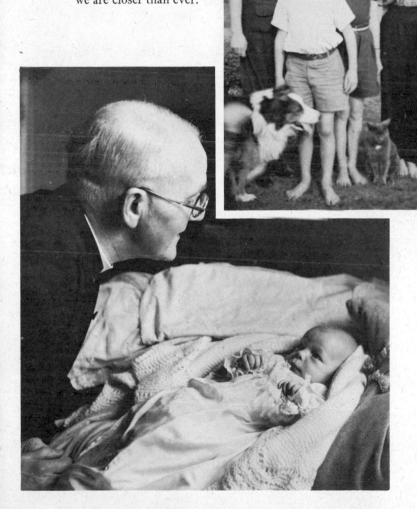

ASPECTS OF LIFE IN STEPNEY. . .

Housewives protest against local housing conditions.

Bystanders watch a Good Friday Procession of Witness in Cable Street. My son Tony is holding the cross.

St. Paul's School receives a visit from H.R.H. Princess Margaret. Both the Princess and her mother have always shown a deep interest in our work.

Wellclose House, Birmingham.

Baptism of a prostitute. "Many who are street women shall go into the Kingdom of God. . ."

Our three wardens Miss Angela Butler and Miss Jean Hodges and Sister E.L. Paskin C.A.

Sisters West and Paskin C.A. outside our Goodmayes House.

Mrs Daphne Morgan and Miss Jean Hodges outside Wellclose
House, London, E.1.

Father Lambert, as he took me out to a simple meal in London. Like old times we climbed to the top of the bus at Burdett Road and got a front seat. Simply and nervously I replied, "I want to be a priest." He must have known how impossible that would be, yet he said, quite simply, "The Vicar of St. Saviour's should be able to help you about that. He was a Chaplain and got the M.C. You are in his parish, go and see him." I read his thoughts and I felt terribly sad and depressed. We got through the evening and I told him I would see the vicar the next morning.

At 11 o'clock the next morning I went to St. Saviour's vicarage, just about 200 yards from my home. The vicar opened the door himself. He was tall and fine-looking, the perfect gentleman. He didn't shake hands, though. He said, "What do you want?" I told him who I was and very, very quietly I said I felt I was called to the Ministry. He looked down at me from a great height, for he had the advantage of the vicarage doorstep as well as his own six foot odd. He said, "How interesting," and I think he said "Good morning." Anyhow, he shut the door.

From the time Father Dawson put me in the choir of St. Saviour's until I went to the war, that vicarage had been the most homely and kindly place in the parish. Many times after my interview with the vicar I saw him and avoided him. I oughtn't to have felt hurt and disappointed, for even an able East End boy must have known that it was almost impossible to realise his vocation in those days, whereas I was raw and very ignorant. To comfort me, my mother said quite simply, "He's not the poor people's parson and won't be here long." She was right.

What a different story it was when Father Lambert arranged an interview for me with Guy Vernon Smith, who was seeing ex-service men who felt they had a vocation. Of course, he couldn't help being charming, but I met him many years later and I gauged from what I saw of him then how generously he must have given me of his best. He questioned and he listened. Had I matriculated, he asked. "You must go to Knutsford Test School, anyhow," he said and he wished me every success. I went from him lighthearted and hopeful. When I got to Knutsford, I recognised the Chief, F. R. Barry, as the Chaplain at Wendover, Halton Park, who had got me out of a court martial for disobeying an order. It gave us a laugh together and as I thought him difficult to talk to it helped a lot. I discovered soon that the Chief was very deaf.

Knutsford Ordination Test School was the old Knutsford Prison and we had the prison cells as our bed-sitter studies. It was a grim place inside and out. Unmarked, except for a number, was the burying ground of those who had been executed since the place was built, along with others, I think, who had died in prison. Very soon the space was dug and flowers set out so that whoever they were and whatever they had done, we showed respect for their bodies while we offered prayers for their souls.

I had a wonderful fifteen months at Knutsford, but I learnt little. My starting point should have been the basic elements of reading, writing, and arithmetic, for I had no grounding in anything. Diving into English Literature, Maths, Greek and History sent my poor mind into a whirl. For a very long period, stretching over more than two terms, I rose at 5 or 5.30 a.m.; a friend, V. R. Hill, tried to help me for some time, but he must have found me a drag. His brain was much more fertile. I tried very, very hard, but all the stuff I tried to assimilate had no relevance to the object of my calling. A certain standard of education was demanded before men could go to a university, to which the top drawer intellectuals were sent. The lesser breed went to the theological colleges. I had just no standard of any kind so there was no place at all for me.

I hardly know why I went on with the entertainment side of the life at Knutsford; perhaps in the back of my mind I hoped the Chief as a special favour would push me through to some nice friend of his, although I don't remember harbouring any such thought. Anyway, our entertainments were good, and for some time I took part in the concert party and dug up all the songs and farces I had performed in the Army. These things I could do fairly well, and I did at one time think I might go into light or musical comedy. Then the other side of life I enjoyed at Knutsford was sport. I could just gain a place in the first XI and sometimes found myself in a Rugby XV.

On the more serious side, the Chief's lectures in the mornings were wonderful; for forty minutes, I think it was, he held the 400 or 500 men spellbound. He made the Acts and the Epistles live, and Paul stood out as a modern man to be understood and appreciated. Nobody has ever made St. Paul live for me like Barry did in his morning lectures at Knutsford.

After morning prayers we had a quarter of an hour of silent meditation in Knutsford Parish Church. How difficult it was for everybody to keep from coughing, blowing their noses, sniffing or rattling their boots. Soft music was tried as well as a healthy blinding from the Vice-Principal, Sykes, but silence at Knutsford was in short supply.

We were all a bit mad, I think. Many of us put on our oldest clothes on Sundays. It was quite cock-eyed for although it was meant as a sign of true fraternity—indifference to dress and outward signs of respectability—we became the centre of attraction which we foolishly enjoyed. To exist at all was a real problem, for although the country paid for our Knutsford keep, there was nothing for vacations. So for four months of the year I had to exist on my 18s. and my poor mother often suffered. It was Father Lambert who kept me going, and I did all the work I could for him in return. It was very often very tough going.

There must have been much good stuff in the lectures I heard, but I could not see what they were meant to do for me and I hadn't the ability to grasp much. I left after fifteen months and was given to understand that I had been given three months or more longer than I should have had. The Chief said, "I am sorry, Willie," and he meant it, I think.

I didn't know what to expect when I went there, but looking back I know what I ought to have had. But none of the staff there thought it possible for any man to be called to the priesthood who, within a year or fifteen months, could not arrive at or near matriculation standard. To my mind there should have been a class for men of my kind and of my limitations. Men who had to start from $2 + 2 = 4$; who needed to be taught the simple form and make up of a sentence; men who could not read. Given two years or three, we should have had a foundation upon which something worthy could have been built. Those who were mistaken about their call would have fallen out through impatience.

What I want to stress is that 100, perhaps 200, were turned away when they ought to have been kept. The Church was screaming for men, but the high-ups were screaming, not for men but for educated rabbits; frightened rabbits, very often. Those of us who were turned down because we couldn't make the grade had something to offer that very, very few of those who passed on to university and to theological college could possibly have had. For the most part we were men who had been, and were, so poor that we could have taken our places by the starving crowds of those years, as priests of understanding, through birth. The Church as a whole had nothing in common with the starving masses of Britain. Those who were turned down intellectually were the men who should have filled the gaps and won the day. So far as Knutsford was concerned, it was a survival of the fittest, the fittest being those who had been fortunate enough, if good fortune it was, to have been to a public school, or to a grammar school. Knutsford was called an Ordination Test School, but it was really an intellectual test school. There may still be doubt in some people's minds as to my vocation, but there is none in my own mind and I think that I may be allowed to say that the proof of my vocation is in the service I have been allowed to give.

The night before I left Knutsford, I went down to the George Inn with a few friends, prepared to do as very many have done, and been sorry for it afterwards: I went to drink and forget. It was a poor effort. I had a glass of beer and then knew that I was a fool.

Going down from Knutsford meant that so far as help was concerned I was finished financially. I had been receiving a Government grant, and when I left Knutsford Barry had to turn the tap off. I asked him to allow me to go to a theological college, but although he was at pains to assure me I was morally fit and that there was nothing against me, he told me quite bluntly that I could not foot the bill intellectually. It was not he who was wrong so much as the whole system. For the intellectual giants of the Church would waste, not be wasted, in the job I have been trying to hold down for the last ten years in Stepney. They would be the first to say, "Every man to his job," but for Williamson they could see no job; "he cannot do maths; he's done no history; no English, no Greek, no Latin; he was brought up in a slum in Poplar, and did any good ever come out of Poplar?" The system was and still is cock-eyed, and it has nothing to do with real vocation. God wanted me, and for a priest. He was not to be frustrated by tinpot people who were running the Church by class distinction, intellectual class distinction.

I don't want to be bitter and I want to be constructive. My bluntness may give offence, but the answer to the question as to who should serve, of men like I was and still am, is a long period of simple, sound teaching.

It is a later story, but I started "free and frank" talks in the Army in the Second World War, before Padre's Hours were thought of (and I suspect that my "free and frank" talks had something to do with the setting up of Padre's Hour). But my point is that when the disciples of Our Lord were told not to bother much about what they were to say when they were up against real opposition, and that the Holy Spirit would tell them what to say, Our Lord meant it. What was wanted of me as an Army Padre was sanctified common sense, in other words, holy wisdom. That first, and then guts, or to be polite, holy courage.

I was never bothered as to what I should say, for having courage to address seventy or eighty soldiers or more and to answer their questions for a couple of hours, I felt no weakness from lack of Greek, Latin or even English grammar. What did help sometimes was to tell the men I was bred and born in East London, and on the few occasions when I was stumped, to tell them, quite candidly, I did not know. But I was to go through many kinds of horrors and fears before I was a stabilised priest.

No sooner had I reached home after seeing Father Lambert than I was offered a job as a travelling gospeller. I could go to Saskatchewan. I would have a caravan. Strangely enough, I have forgotten who offered me this job. Anyhow, it did not materialise, but quite suddenly I seemed to have become someone. For almost immediately Father Jenks, S.S.M. sent for me and told me I should be most unhappy if I went to that part of Canada. He pressed me to go to Melanesia. I knew nothing of those places, but did not mind where I went so long as it might lead me where I was meant to go.

Father Jenks put me into touch with a Father Corner, the Commissary to the Bishop of Melanesia. I saw Father Corner in London, and there was no doubt that he wanted me. He was a gracious, middle-aged priest. Quite suddenly, when I thought nearly everything was settled, he gave me a quick look, straight in the eye, and said, "Would you like to go to a good college for a year?" From the depth of my very soul I said, "I should love it." I got a second shock, because he said, "You can go to any college you like," and he looked as if he could have sent me to any college in England. What did I know about colleges? Apart from hearing many colleges mentioned at Knutsford, and being "Oxford" during the weeks before the Boat Race, because Father Dawson was Oxford, I knew nothing about such places. "Where would you advise me to go, sir?" I asked. He replied, "St. Augustine's College, Canterbury." "Let me go there, sir, for a year, and thank you."

Strange as it may seem, I do not remember where this took place and I never saw Father Corner again. It seemed that I was being passed on from one person to the other.

I stayed at St. Augustine's for four years, and I loved nearly every minute I spent there. Bishop Knight, formerly of Rangoon, was the Warden. He was a splendid person and a saint. I gave him some bad times and I might easily have been turned down. He could shame me without speaking, and my loud-mouthed gestures, a Cockney weakness, he shook off with a sigh. There were no tricks about him, he was honest and clean cut all through. He was one of a very scholarly family and a very, very poor one. We were told many times, as an illustration of his poverty, how he had no trunk or leather bag, and took his luggage to Cambridge in a wooden box and carted it on a railway barrow from the station to Caius, his college. When we were uppish and showing off, he would put out his hand and move it up and down, keeping time with his Greek words: "*Tepi nosis, tepi nosis*." He would then interpret the Greek for us: "Keep humble, keep humble." He would say these words in a special kind of voice, a voice he never used for anything else; it began on a top note, swooped down and ended on a note which made it a question and before you realised it you were saying, "Yes, sir."

The great man set us essays, and when we went to him he sat us on a low stool on the right side of his chair, a position which gave him more than a fair advantage. I didn't mind going to him to be put through it, for he was delightfully simple and he always helped me to put my many mistakes right.

He was a great walker and moved at great speed. One of us would be collected at 2.15 and dashed through the countryside with him until 4 o'clock. But at the end of it was a delicious tea with his invalid sister, Minnie. I didn't do much walking with the Warden because I was useful enough to be needed at soccer and cricket.

He was, of course, very strict about our association with girls; there was to be none of it, though there had been a marriage or two in years past, before men had got through to Ordination. In spite of this, some of us went out with some delightful nurses at the Kent and Canterbury Hospital.

We took our first-aid and watched good surgeons operate at the hospital as part of our training. We also went round the wards with the surgeons and did casualty duty. A pretty face was sometimes more interesting than a surgical knife being pressed into a body, and a cut finger could be managed much better with a second person around, especially if she were attractive. When she was nice the distance between the hospital and a teashop was just nothing, so some of us got very friendly with the nurses.

We had some rather good rags at St. Augustine's. One or two are worth recording. The College is only just off the site and ruins of the old Abbey with its walls 6 to 8 feet thick. Under a moon on a clear night the ruins looked eerie; lifeless, yet full of ghostly quiet life. There was a look of sanctity about the place and the shadows were various and odd. So for a night duty sister at the hospital, middle-aged and slightly nervous, there were things to be seen when she glanced down at the ruins in the quiet of the night. The sister confided in one of our special staff nurse friends and she confided in us, and so some real ghosts were arranged. I wonder if the Bishop of the Upper Nile remembers how he and I climbed out of the College grounds with white sheets at a few minutes to mid-night. He went to one end of the ruined Abbey and I went to the other. George Appleton, now Archdeacon of London, was to keep watch inside the College and to warn us by whistling in case of danger. Perfectly covered from head to foot, like ghostly monks, with hoods pointed, we began to walk towards each other from opposite ends of the Abbey wall. It was at the first stroke of mid-night that we started our long, dignified, slow walk with one fore-arm out in front. The Kent and Canterbury Hospital ran parallel with the Abbey ruins. As we made our way we heard chuckles through the silent night. The nurses had seen us. So had the nervous night sister. Ginger Wilson and I met at the tombs of the archbishops, abbots and other honoured men. After looking into the tombs we walked together to the East and into the lower ruins. There we quickly changed and made our way to where a ladder was placed against the wall. But we had to wait for the all-clear whistle from George and all we got was a danger whistle. It was cold and we were tired. After a longish time the gentle all clear came. We wanted no second bidding, we were over and through the cloisters in no time to join George.

Why were we kept out? It was Ted again. Ted was a very keen scout and hated being kept in the dark about anything. He was generally clever enough to find out what was going on, but in the process he called attention to the fact that something was in the wind, so that the Sub-Warden always caught the scent. The Sub-Warden was also of a curious nature, and on this occasion had come from his rooms and lingered about the spot where we must return. It was late when we got back, but not so late that we could not hold a trial on Ted. He had no defence, so we tied him up and took him down to the lavatory tap and turned the water on and soddened him from head to foot. Even that didn't cure his curiosity.

But what was happening in the hospital? The sister knew who was playing the joke on her and she flew down the stairs into the young house surgeon's bedroom. The doctor slept with his head submerged, and without hesitation she went to the top of the bed and pulled back the clothes. The doctor thought she was mad; she was so shocked that she was unable to speak, and the doctor called a staff nurse to look after her. It was a good rag and nearly everything went as it should.

With the best but the most gruesome of all rags I had nothing to do, except to enjoy it. Usher and Bodger were the two clever people concerned. They staged murder in the College. Or was it suicide? They made up a dead Usher covered with blood. It was the most natural dummy I have ever seen, and deceived members of the staff as well as most of the men. The live Usher sat under his own desk seeing and hearing everything. Bodger acted very cleverly. White-faced and shaken he quietly took people in and said, "We mustn't touch anything until the police and the doctor have been; he's quite dead." I was entirely deceived. And I saw a nervous and very, very High Church and spiky student kneel pathetically and cross himself reverently. Nearly every member of the College was taken in and the rag lasted two or three hours.

When it was decided that I should go on at the College to complete full training for the priesthood, instead of going to Melanesia, the Warden took me more under his wing. He must have had many doubts about me. Thinking back, I picture myself asserting myself, putting my neck right out. I had no reserve, no real wish to be quiet. I tried to read and to assimilate and couldn't; the knowledge did not become a part of me, and was quickly forgotten. Even now I have not acquired the art of taking notes.

As I was floundering along to my ordination, without a foundation of elementary knowledge, lecturers were naturally far in advance of my understanding. They would use a word which I would jot down so that, on the quiet, I could seek its meaning from my bosom friend, the dictionary. But in thinking of the word I would miss a whole line of thought. On one such occasion the Sub-Warden was lecturing on Ezekiel. I asked him a question which he thought stupid. He was very caustic, and his sarcasm raised the intended laugh against me from the other students. Unhappily I turned to him and told him that sarcasm didn't help much. I knew I would be for it. After lecture I joined him and apologised. He met me graciously and murmured that it might have been his fault. I hardly know what made me go on, but I said, "Do you know the answer to sarcasm in Poplar?" He said no. I told him a punch on the nose. He said nothing; my rudeness and pugnacity were taken well.

Without doubt I was given the length of a very long rope at St. Augustine's and every allowance must have been made for my up-bringing. I felt my position less then than I do now, in retrospect, yet intellectually I must have been a borderline case and my vocation might easily have been in question. But just as being a "Blue" helps a graduate who may not be very bright at study, so I think my ability to play and teach soccer may have gained me sympathy from the staff at St. Augustine's. I captained a poor, but willing XI for three years.

My ear began to give me pain half-way through my course. The college doctor made an appointment for me with a London surgeon who visited the Kent and Canterbury Hospital one Sunday a month. A single examination of my ear and head told him that I must have an operation without delay. I went into the hospital, and it was a joy to know everybody there, from the matron down-wards, and the house doctors were friends too.

Operations thirty-eight years ago weren't quite what they are today. I had seen this mastoid operation go wrong; I had seen people with good features come out of the operation with their mouths twisted to one side of their faces, crippled in speech and with their appearance ruined for life. Yet I went into it light-heartedly. Before the surgeon arrived I was on the table chatting to the house surgeon. He challenged me to sing a song, which I did, to the amusement of nurses and doctor. Not longer than five minutes from that time everyone in the theatre was working to save my life, so the story goes, for I very nearly went out before the operation started.

Hundreds of doctors and specialists have admired the work of that surgeon on my ear and head, but since that time I have had some very bad spasms. I have sometimes felt I couldn't go on because of pain and noises in the head.

The examinations came thick and heavy after my operation. The results were poor indeed, yet somehow I was allowed to continue and continue until I arrived for my Deacon's examination for ordination. I had seen the Bishop of London, and I had seen the Vicar of a church in Middlesex, who had given me a "title", which meant that he took me to work in his parish to begin my ministry.

At my Deacon's examination two things stand out, my inability to cope and feel satisfied with any question on the paper, and a very long interview in the middle of that examination with a Canon Eck, the Bishop's examining chaplain. He was meant to give me a bit of unseen Greek, but instead he made me talk. He was a most gracious man.

There was much rejoicing in Poplar when it was known that Joe Williamson was to be ordained. I hadn't a bean, and it was my dearest friend and spiritual father who bought everything for me. Father Lambert must have spent £30 to £40 on me before my ordination. In 1925 that was a lot of money.

The actual ordination was like a dream, it was so strange and wonderful. Dear Winnington Ingram was always most kind to me. I am quite sure that no other bishop would have ordained me, and I am equally sure that his affection for Father Lambert influenced him, together with a letter from my dear Warden, Bishop Knight. Still, to me it was a miracle. My mother shed tears nearly all the time, according to my sister, and if I know anything about Doll, she did much the same. My mother was so much in heaven that when she made her Communion she forgot to take her gloves off and the Bishop had to ask her to remove them before communicating her.

CHAPTER VIII

Ordination to the Priesthood

THE first two years of my ministry were for the most part sheer hell for me and others. I want so badly to put this clearly and fairly. To do that I must give a picture of the Church of England and its clergy in 1925, and the contrast I made to the general set-up.

On the whole the clergy were respected and feared. As a body they belonged to the privileged classes, being gentlemen by birth and education. Real education was a closed shop and a formidable barrier separated the haves and have-nots. Against every kind of social convention I was put into this privileged band.

For the first year of my ministry I was neither acceptable nor accepted, and the year, a terrible one for me, ended tragically. The Bishop of London had asked me to go to a church in Middlesex, where the vicar offered me a title. I was there expressly to work in a very poor area.

The Bishop thought, quite properly, that I would be useful in such a neighbourhood because I was "one of them". Unfortunately, the vicar proved a wrong choice. He was not a man of strict discipline himself, and could not help me. This was very bad for me, for I needed discipline and a great deal of kindly guidance, and I got neither. The vicar saw me only when he had to. I needed to have my sermons corrected, being so bad at expressing myself; but after he had looked at one or two of them it was obvious that I could be of little interest to him. I realised only too well that I was the wrong person for him.

One evening the vicar was late at evensong. He was to read the lessons and preach, and I was to sing the service. He had not appeared by the first lesson, so I made my way to the lectern and started to read. My name being Joseph, the lesson just had to be the story of Joseph and Potiphar's wife. I could indeed have seen that through decently, had the vicar not come puffing in when I was half-way through. He realised what lesson I was reading and then and there in front of the congregation made gestures of despair. I said at once, "Here endeth the first lesson" and gave out the office hymn.

Because I really was "one of them", people outside the church as well as in began to take to me, and to compare me with my chief. This was fatal to me in nearly every way. The worst was in my feeling of importance and superiority. I imagined I was somebody, and sadly bungled the whole difficult situation.

There was a very good Scout troop attached to the church and the Scoutmaster was a very efficient man. I went to the poor area and knocked at every door afternoon after afternoon. I got as many as fifty lads together, many without boots or proper clothes. These were the lads who needed the Church and the help of the Church most, and I thought we should make Scouts of them. I pleaded for money and got all I wanted. But the Scoutmaster did not want the tough boys with his nice Scouts. I spoke to the vicar about it and he sided with the Scoutmaster. I was told to form a separate troop, and I tried hard, but the poor kids just weren't wanted. It was a horrible and sad business. I felt hopelessly lost. I hated the Scoutmaster and disliked the vicar. I nearly ran away. I was terribly lonely.

Nearing Easter I thought seriously of my confession, and felt I must put things right with the Scoutmaster. I told him I was about to make my confession and that I had hated him and it was wrong of me. Stupidly I thought he might respond but not a bit of it. He just said, "That's all right." He was a man of excellent education with a very good home and was conscious of his superiority.

While I was feeling depressed and frustrated I discovered that some people looked up to me. It had never occurred to me that I should be regarded as someone above the ordinary. Finding myself

on a pedestal at the very time when I was humiliated and emotionally warped, I began to cultivate the good opinion of those who
sympathised with me against the vicar.

About this time there were quite a few robberies in the area,
and a member of the church, an old spinster, became nervous
because she had a big house and lived alone. I went to see the old
lady, and I must have been some comfort to her. To hold my
interest the poor soul wanted to give me all sorts of presents. I
would not take a thing, but I used to call in and have the odd cup
of tea. She told me that none of her nieces or nephews wrote to her
or came near to her and it soon became clear that she was centring
her affection on me. My history made her want to do something
for me. Here, I felt, was more trouble; my vicar would think I was
getting something out of the old lady. I called on Miss Smith less
and less, and she upset herself more and more. It was a tragic
situation for there was nothing wrong about her interest. I did
allow her to give me one present. "You may give me the best
Priest's Service Book that money can buy and it will last me all my
days." This she loved doing, and it was and still is a most lovely
book. Very modestly she put her initials and the date in the corner
of the first page.

I often wish I could have dealt more wisely with the situation,
but when I left the area a few months later I determined to drop
her absolutely. It was terribly sad, for I used to see her walking near
my flat in my new parish. My heart ached for her, but I did not
want her bothering me.

She died suddenly six months after I left my first job, and she
left me nearly £3,000. There were conditions, one being that I
should conduct the burial service. I did conduct it, in the face of all
her relatives. They thought her money should have gone to them and
that I had done them out of it; yet I had done more for her than they,
and that was precious little. I had known nothing of Miss Smith's
intentions. Had I done so, would I have been kinder to her?

There was a further condition to the gift, which I was unable to
carry out. The condition does not matter, but where the the money
was to go in the event of my not being able to fulfil her wishes
matters greatly. It was like a delightful fairy story. My mother,

who had slaved all her life and who went into service at nine years of age, inherited the money by default. I had told Miss Smith of Mother's work, goodness, and self-sacrifice, and of my own call. She made her will. She tried to tie me down. If that failed then my mother must benefit.

When I received the solicitor's letter notifying me that the money and certain bits of furniture were mine, I made arrangements at my bank to raise enough money to give my mother what she had always longed for; a cottage in the country. At that time she wasn't too well, and felt overcrowded in Hill Place Street, Poplar. I told her what I was going to do and she wept with gratitude. I felt a bit full.

My good friend Father Lambert was called in to help. Knowing the country and what it can be like in winter compared with Poplar with neighbours on your doorstep all the year round, we thought of a country place with some life in it. We went to Benfleet, which was a biggish village and with the Thames in sight. As luck would have it, nice little brick houses were being erected and I bought one for £800. I moved my mother and a young nephew down to the cottage. I kept in close touch to see that all was well, and for a week or two things seemed to go happily. But on one of my weekly visits I saw that Mother was far from well. I took my nephew for a little walk and asked him to tell me exactly what was wrong. Very sadly he told me that Mother wanted to go back to Poplar. It was so quiet she couldn't sleep, and there was no one to talk to. "Come on," I said to Will, "we'll soon put this right." I am certain she would not have lived much longer had I not got her back to East London. She was simply homesick. Very gently I approached her about it, and she wept. Happily my sister was still in the old house in Poplar. We were packed and back in London in a day.

It took some time to get Mother back to normal, because she felt she had let me down. After that she settled for the rest of her days in Poplar, leaving it, apart from holidays, only for two weeks during the war. It was her home.

When she found that she had inherited money, she went to the solicitor and asked him why she had got it. She then asked if there was any reason why she should not give it to me, seeing she was an old woman and I had always looked after her and would do so until

she died. She made the money over to me without touching it. I
in turn had a document drawn up legally giving her the interest
on two-thirds of the capital until her death.

She lived until she was seventy-nine. Up to within two years of
her death she was as energetic as ever, and even then, in spite of
high blood pressure, she continued to keep fit by resting properly
and taking her pills. The end came suddenly, in September 1942.
She was taken ill in the early afternoon, having prepared and cooked
the dinner as usual. Later she became unconscious and she died
at 7 o'clock. My sister Doll, who had lived with her all her life except
for five or six years, was with her at the end. I was in Gibraltar, and
Father Lambert did everything for me, and for his old friend Lucy.
Father Bartlett, Vicar of St. Saviour's, and also an old friend of
Mother's, wrote to me and among other things said, "Lucy
Williamson had her purgatory here on earth."

In retrospect, her funeral was not without its amusing side,
although it was no joke for the mourners in attendance. As it was
wartime, petrol consumption had to be watched carefully. The
hearse was well supplied and, like Elijah's chariot, it flew on and
away. The car bearing poor Father Lambert and the mourners
stuck. They had run out of petrol. I cannot help thinking that
Mother would have enjoyed the joke.

My mother was particularly close to me during the difficult first
two years of my ministry. She suffered terribly with me, and I
could almost feel her prayers for me.

It came as a shock to be told, on the very morning that I was to
go to Fulham Palace for retreat before my priesthood, that I was
not suitable for the selected parish.

It happened this way. A month or so before I was due to be
ordained priest, I asked the vicar if I might say my first mass in
Poplar, and without hesitation he said yes. The morning of my
departure, I was at mass. Quite politely, I approached the priest's
vestry and said I had to be off to Fulham Palace after breakfast. I
thought he hadn't heard, so I went on, "I go into retreat today for
my ordination." He turned away and grunted. More politely I
went on, "You very kindly said that I might say my first mass in

Poplar, is that all right, Father?" He turned furiously and said, "No, it isn't and I have told the Bishop that you are entirely unfit for work in this parish." He was a big man and he made as if to go out of the door. I put my heel to it and told him what I thought of him. Not a word had he spoken to me on the subject, and he would have allowed me to go to Fulham knowing nothing of his letter. He said he had never been spoken to in such a way before. I told him he had been sadly neglected, but he was getting it this morning.

I left him then, thinking I was entirely finished. The Bishop would not overlook this, and anyhow I had no parish and he could not therefore ordain me.

I arrived at the Palace and saw the Chaplain who went to the Bishop, and the Bishop saw me at once. He was very kind, but I said, "When you have heard what has happened you won't be so kind." He heard me out, and then said, "I understood from your vicar that you both agreed that you were not suitable." I told him that we had not spoken on the subject until that morning. He told me to go in with the other ordinands while he sent for my vicar. Later he sent for me again and said he wanted us both to walk in the garden and make peace. We went into the garden and I tried to talk to my vicar and reach a basis of understanding. I asked him to take me for three months so that I could be priested. He would not consent, and at last I said, "This is a waste of time, let's get back to the Bishop." The Bishop sent me away again, but soon he came to me and said, "I want you to apologise to Father . . . for your conduct this morning." I said I would apologise most sincerely. In front of the Bishop, the Archdeacon and the Bishop's Chaplain I said I was sorry and asked my vicar to forgive me. The Bishop also urged him to forgive me and to take me back, but sad to say he refused. The Bishop was furious. I was sacked, but the Bishop ordained me priest although I had no job.

It was a terrible time. The Bishop sent for Father Lambert and told him to look after me following my ordination and to arrange things for me; Father Lambert went and collected my pay.

I eventually went as assistant curate to Father Haynes at St. James, Norland Square. Haynes was a dear man but he showed

H

no inclination to train me. I was set to work in the slum area of the parish, and I had a flat in Alfred House over the Sunday market which began to open up at 5 o'clock on Sunday mornings. The pubs kept open until midnight, after which fights invariably started. There were cheap and filthy doss houses a few yards away.

The church was well situated, surrounded on three sides by very good houses, and there seemed no lack of money. Behind the church was a different story. This was the country of the poor, and the farther back you went the worse it got. A redeeming feature was the very fine church hall in the back street area. I started a club for the youngsters of my own sort. Boxing was the favourite pastime. Since my operation I had been sensitive to the slightest touch in the region of the ear and now I was trying to teach boxing. No sooner had I begun than a tall and strong lad was very anxious to have the gloves on with me. I was Cockney enough to sense trouble, and suggested he should help to teach, but he didn't want that. So I took him on. He was very strong and was out to do the curate, and I began to wonder how long I should last before getting a clout on the side of my head. Somehow I got through safely but I knew I was foolish and if I kept on it was only a matter of time. The best solution would be to put someone in my place. This I did in the shape of my young nephew, Will. He was only about sixteen at the time, but he had won an amateur final after seven or eight contests. He was very light and small but he moved like lightning in the ring. To put him in for three rounds with the lad who was trying so hard to down me would be slaughter for Will if he was caught. I warned him of the danger, but he pulled off the encounter brilliantly. He never got hit but landed blows when and where he liked. He went on teaching for me for some months.

I thoroughly enjoyed my club and Father Haynes, the vicar, took a deep interest in that too. I stayed at St. James for nearly two years.

I have often said that my wife was my best investment. In only a few months we had met and married. It was the greatest surprise to Audrey when I asked her to marry me, for I had shown no sign of affection at all, and neither had she. It took two or three days for her to get over the shock of the proposal, and I thought it was off;

but it was gloriously on, and plans were made for the wedding on All Saints' Day, 1927.

It was a bit trying for her relations, who were kindly but county; her father was a doctor in Petworth. My people didn't exactly fit the bill and perhaps I didn't either. I was very glad when the wedding was over. We went to Lodsworth for our honeymoon and then on to Bognor to do a temporary job before we sailed for South Africa on 7th January 1928.

There is no doubt at all in my mind that the next twenty-five years of my ministry were leading up to my return to the East End of London. I spent some years in South Africa, then, having tried and failed to get a church in St. Helena, I was offered the Rectory of Fenny Drayton near Nuneaton. The rectory had twenty-three rooms and the water had to be pumped from outside. During the eighteen months we were there, we made the place habitable, but nevertheless we were relieved when, out of blue, there came the offer of the parishes of Shimpling and Alpheton in the diocese of St. Edmundsbury and Ipswich.

Early in 1940 I went into the Army as a chaplain. My war experiences, especially the years spent in Gibraltar, were a valuable preparation for my later work, as I had dealings with all types and classes of men.

I could happily have remained at Shimpling all my days and been very comfortable, but I knew I was meant to move on, and three years after leaving the Army I moved to Sporle and Little Dunham in West Norfolk. It was here, in 1952, that I received a postcard from an old friend, the Rev. C. L. B. Brown, who was Tubby Clayton's right-hand man. It said simply: "It's about time you returned to London. St. Paul's, Dock Street, is vacant. I have put your name forward."

PART TWO

STEPNEY

CHAPTER I

Return to East London

I CAME to Stepney in 1952.

Previous to my interview with the Trustees of the living, Mr. Canham, the churchwarden, travelled to see me at Sporle. He and his wife had lived in the schoolkeeper's house at St. Paul's School in Wellclose Square for many years. They were an excellent couple, simple, old-fashioned church people. Mr. Canham wanted to give me the once-over as a likely candidate for the living of St. Paul's.

My hopes of returning to London had faded years before, and now, with the possibility suddenly at hand, I naturally used all my guile to get this appointment. But Canham was not the sort of man to be satisfied with letters. He wanted to come and see me in my own parish. He was a Norfolk man himself, and loved Norfolk, and he could not see why I should want to leave such a beautiful place for the drabness of East London. For we did have a lovely home, with a beautiful garden which my wife had made, and a good tennis-court. Why did I want to leave it all? It was a hard question to answer. But I had to persuade Mr. Canham to want me as Vicar of St. Paul's.

We went to London to see the parish. Audrey did not like it a bit, and I could see that I would need all my energy to cope with it. After a succession of country parishes, it was gloomy and depressing. The vicarage, though large and roomy, was dismal and quite uninviting. There was no garden. The church was in a very bad state of repair, literally black, and badly lit. But this was beyond doubt where God wanted me to be.

We moved in just before Christmas. The first thing to do was to set about beautifying the church, and without the generosity of the Diocese it could never have been done. The Bishop of Stepney was ready to give me all the help he could. The collections were poor, around £2. 10s. 0d. a Sunday, the congregation only forty to fifty strong. The roof badly needed mending for a start. When it rained, every possible receptacle was used to catch the water. Every penny we could spare was put into a Restoration Fund, which the Queen Mother opened with a generous donation—just one of the many gracious acts of kindness she has shown to the parish. The ship weathervane on the church steeple—St. Paul's is known as the Seamen's Church, and was built in the middle of the last century in connection with the Sailors' Home—had to come down for cleaning and regilding, and before it was put back I took it round the parish on wheels to help to raise money for the Fund.

The parish of St. Paul's, Dock Street, lies just east of the City, with Commercial Road to the north, the Tower and the Royal Mint to the west, and Wapping and the Docks to the south. Dock Street itself, where the church and vicarage and the new Red Ensign Club building stand, is a fairly wide and clean street. But turn off beside the railway bridge into Cable Street and you are at once in a world of crowded tenements, sordid cafés, bomb sites, and narrow alleys lined with buildings which should have been pulled down years ago. Many of the old type houses in the area have one tap, and one lavatory in the yard, and these serve for eight or nine sets of people, the rooms being let out separately to families or individuals.

This area is the breeding ground for vice of every description, where in recent years evil and unscrupulous men have moved in with their all-night cafés and their brothels, making life hell for the decent people who have to bring up children in the midst of all these horrors.

Behind Cable Street is Wellclose Square, which was to become the centre for the most important part of my work in Stepney. Here stands the church school, where the children at least can receive Christian teaching that will help them to stand against the evils around them. And here too is Church House, which later became a refuge for some of the hundreds of prostitutes in this area. But I had not received the challenge that was to bring this work into being.

My hope when I first came to Stepney was to model my parish on the one I had known as a boy, and where I had first received my call to the priesthood: St. Saviour's, Poplar.

Perhaps because of these memories, I took a particular interest in the church schools, which were always a great joy to me. I welcomed the chance to teach young children to worship and pray. Many people, I know, think that a weekly Sung Eucharist is inappropriate for children. They argue that children can have little or no understanding of either the actions or the words. But to my mind it is like learning the Lord's Prayer, or being taught about the Fatherhood of God, the saving power of Jesus and the guidance of the Holy Spirit. They are indeed just words, words, words at first, but the time may come when the words acquire reality and then they mean life, and worship, and prayer. To join in the Mass sung in English can be a great and valuable habit for children. No matter how young they are, it becomes a part of them. If we don't do these things with them, they may never have a chance to learn anything about them, and there are so many other things that will soon fill their minds. So I taught these children to sing the Mass to the music of Merbeck, in faith that the repetition of the words of worship, confession and prayer would bring something to life in the heart and soul of some Stepney boy or girl, as they did for me in Poplar many years ago.

Another special activity, modelled on the St. Saviour's of my childhood, was the Good Friday procession of witness. On my first Good Friday, I led a procession of twenty-five into the parish. Every year since then the witness has grown until it has become a Deanery procession, and we visit the worst parts of Stepney, with as many as 200 people taking part. We preach, we pray, and we recite the Creed as we walk through the streets. I am sure this is the way the Litany was meant to be sung. With its petitions, its responses and its silences it creates the right frame of mind in the participants, and the watchers remain silent too. Then, saying the Lord's Prayer, the Creed and the Gloria, keeps the mind attentive and keeps the minds of the listeners focused on the spirit which moves us. We have even silenced the Cable Street juke boxes, and claimed the reverent attention of the toughest characters. Drama forces the message home: I have found myself on my knees in the gutter of Cable Street, demonstrating how the Lord washed the dirty feet of His disciples. I have pleaded for mercy and forgiveness at the foot of the crude wooden Cross which we carry. Then as many as eight or nine in the procession, lay men and women and priests, will speak to the watching people.

This was the more spectacular side of my work. For the most part it was the ordinary routine of any parish priest—hospital visiting, caring for those who needed care, meeting people and speaking to them, feeding the hungry, marrying the young couples and baptising their babies. I worked like a slave, visited regularly, pleaded and begged people to return to Church. I would not baptise children without the most careful instruction of the parents. Saturday evenings I devoted to the instruction of young couples in Christian marriage, and the bringing of God into their home. They accepted it all happily—yet after marriage, with few exceptions, they sank into themselves, content with the TV and the bed. They would come to me again when the children arrived, and I would again try to reach them through the baptism, along the lines of "Where you want this child to go you must lead the way." For the most part the response was nil. This disappointment is something every priest knows. The superstition is as common in Park Lane as it is in Poplar or Stepney about baptism and perhaps Holy Communion. Try as we will to make these Sacraments a real link with God and nourishment for good living, we still seem to fail. For most people the Church has its place, for baptism as for marriage, but there is too often no interest in regular worship.

Perhaps the best thing about these talks was that we got to know each other. I have made it my business to get to know as many people as possible in the parish, whether they come to church or not. I try not to pass anyone by in the street without a greeting, and they all know "Father Joe". Many are my friends. Others openly hate me, but at least they can't say the Church ignores them. There are the toughs who run the cafés. There are the prostitutes. There are the methylated spirit drinkers, the drug takers, the bums. And there are the many respectable working people trying to keep up a decent standard amongst all the squalor.

In this setting, the work would have been impossible without my family's solid support. My three children, Joy, Lucy and Tony, have always been a tremendous joy to me, and we have been very close. We trust each other absolutely. Audrey and I had shown our confidence in them in a very practical way when they were still quite young. Just before I went overseas in the war, I sold up my small investments, and divided the money into three. I took the children along to the post office and opened an account for each of them. From that date they paid their own school fees and bought everything they needed, knowing that that was all the money there was, and that if they wasted it, there was no more. I have never regretted this. I believe that children should be trusted, and put in a position of trust.

They in their turn knew they could rely on our help when they needed it. As they grew up, I assured them, they would encounter difficulties and get into trouble. When these things happened, no matter how bad they seemed, they could come to us, who loved them most of all, and we would always be kind and understanding. I am sure that the very fact that they can talk things over with Audrey and me without fear has given them added confidence in themselves. It works the other way round, too. This frank understanding has made me pause, when I am in a bad temper, which happens all too often, and wonder what they would think of me. Now they are grown up, they do not hesitate to say what they feel. If anything, we are closer today, though they have left home and have families of their own, than we have ever been.

Audrey, of course, has always been a great help to me, and particularly in these last few years. When women and girls, hearing of our work, have called at the vicarage asking for help, she has asked them in and entertained them. If for some reason they have not wanted to go to Church House, or there has been no room for them, she has put them up, treating them as one of the family. Our home was once the perfect hiding-place for a girl who was being looked for by every authority in the area; but we have always escaped the frowns of the law, mainly, I am sure, because of my wife's disarming charm.

It is Audrey who notes down my appointments, remembers important facts and dates, and is generally my eyes and ears. She has written thousands of letters for me, and has been my most perfect unpaid overworked secretary. Before I had a staff she seemed to do everything, and run the house too. She has shared in all my work and suffered its disappointments and its rewards. She is never irritated, always easy-going. The whole neighbourhood, even the worst thugs, revere her.

She has only one failing, and that is a good one. When she has fallen for a hard-luck story, and opened her purse, she has met me with, "I'm afraid I have done it again!" We have both been taken in many times, but my instructions have been very definite about giving to scroungers—that we can't afford to be done twice.

Apart from my family, I had a great help at the time of settling in, in the saintly Admiral Padre Woods. He was well over sixty, physically frail, but strong in faith and prayer. At the age of fifty he had retired from the Navy and had been ordained. The whole of his ministry was spent as Chaplain to the Sailor's Home and Red Ensign Club in Dock Street. He lived in the club, and from there he visited in the parish and helped me in St. Paul's Church. He was crippled, so it was more convenient for us to say Mattins and Mass each day in his little chapel. The old padre had a great sense of humour, and lots of wisdom. One day my wife and he were talking outside the vicarage when one of our girls went past. She wished them "good morning", and the Padre asked who she was. Audrey told him. "Isn't that the girl we are praying for?" he wanted to know. She replied that it was. "Pretty girl that," he remarked. "I must pray harder." His religious life was one with his normal life, simple, happy and loving. I always enjoyed his company.

The Padre's position in the parish was a little peculiar. He was not a regular curate, but a voluntary assistant and was supposed to get £5 a year, though I only learned of this just before his death in 1954, when he suddenly asked me why he didn't get his £5. He was always extremely generous to the church, in gifts of money and in many other ways. He used to visit regularly in the parish, and the people all loved him. He loved to take the Parish Communion at 10 a.m., and we had a small altar put in the nave to make it easier for him. A few weeks after I came to the parish, I was urged to sing the Parish Communion, because I had a good voice and the holy padre hadn't. I fell for it, and the next Sunday I took that service and he sat out. I realised later how deeply this had hurt him, and I allowed him to sing that service, the most important one, whenever he could. The daily Masses we took in turns, and I always served for him.

Padre Woods died on All Saints' Day, 1954. He was sadly missed in the parish, especially by all those people who had known his encouragement and comfort during the hard days of the blitz. It was he who had had the idea that the new east window in the church should be dedicated as a memorial to those who had lost their lives in the parish during the war. With his death I was determined that it should also be a memorial to this great and humble man, who had served these people so faithfully. This was done, and the Memorial window was unveiled by the Queen Mother on the 23rd April 1956.

Besides the Padre, I had two official assistant curates. Gordon Budd came to the parish with his wife in December 1953. He too had been in the Navy for many years, and was above the usual age for a theological student. He came to me as a deacon, and they moved into poor accommodation in Chamber Street. Among other things he started a young people's club which was a great success. He was very useful with his hands, and there was little he did not know about electrical fittings, a useful accomplishment at this particular time, with the restoration of the church going on. Among other things he beautifully restored the broken figures of our Christmas Crib. His wife also was a great help. Besides running the junior side of the club, she was Sacristan for practically the whole time of their stay in the parish. They were with us until September 1955.

Then the Bishop sent me Sammy Johnson, a young Nigerian who had been adopted by St. Martin-in-the-Fields. He stayed for nearly three years, after which he went to London University to study for his B.D. When he graduated, his friends at St. Paul's bought him his hood. Sammy was very popular in the parish. He was good at visiting, he ran a club, and he played cricket and football with the very youngest as well as the oldest, to the great joy of parents who eagerly watched his prowess. He lived at the vicarage, and was like a son to me. Every morning early we were on parade together for worship and prayer.

This early morning time of worship is at the heart of our work—Mattins at 7 o'clock followed by preparation and Mass, followed by private prayer and meditation until 8.30. Any unsteadiness and uncertainty in my spiritual life has come from slipping up in this habit; happily for me and the work, these times have been few. I have tried to get my small staff together more often than this for prayer, but the work has got in the way of it. There may be those who feel that the prayers are more important. God will judge whether the act of helping a girl in trouble, taking another to hospital, finding a job for another, is more important than spending our time in prayer in words. The prayers of our little group take the form of practical, compassionate help, and this goes on for very many hours a day.

We have our lighter moments. A West Indian, a particular friend of ours, was continually in and out of a mental hospital. He would discharge himself, and when he was in a bad state he would come back to us for help. One day he came to ask Nora Neal, my lady worker, if she could let him have some old clothes for his children. Nora said she thought she could help, if he would give her a list of their names and ages. Presently he came back with a list of twenty-four names. We have never to this day discovered whether they were in fact all his, but we are quite prepared to believe that they are. But whatever his personal failings, our friend can be very righteous about the morals of other people. He turned up on my doorstep late one night, with an enormous middle-aged prostitute in tow, and a small, bewildered-looking West Indian boy of about nineteen. "Father," he said, sternly, "you've got to make him marry her!" The poor boy looked scared stiff, but obviously resigned to going through with it. I took him on one side and whispered: "Now's your chance. Run for it, I'm on your side." He shot me a grateful look and disappeared quickly down the street while I talked my friend out of it. Sadly, we have a great many of these mentally weak characters in Stepney. Little can be done for them, for they refuse to stay in hospital. We help them all we can, but they are a real problem.

Much of my time was taken up with visiting. I used to try to call on five or six families a day. If the television was on, I would usually sit and watch the programme through with them, but sometimes I would be bold enough to say, "Turn that off, I've got something much more important to say," and they would usually listen to me quite willingly.

It was when I was visiting in the Peabody Buildings opposite the vicarage, one Christmas Day soon after I came to the parish, that I discovered another great problem, that of the old people.

I called on eighty-year-old Mrs Few, a particular pet of mine, and a loyal member of my small congregation. She opened the door to me, and I had to apologise at once, for I had disturbed her at her Christmas dinner. "I've got a chop," she told me, "but it's a poor one." I took the chop in my hands and it was like a piece of india-rubber. I threw it straight on the fire. The old lady looked at me in astonishment, and protested: "Now I've got no dinner at all." As I reassured her, I found my thoughts running away from her to others like her in my parish, and I inwardly vowed that all those lonely old people would have a real Christmas dinner next year.

The more I went into the facts, the more determined I was, for I found that the Home Helps, who come to the old people every day, quite naturally have their days off at Christmas, so the old people are left for perhaps three or four days to fend for themselves.

Now every year before Christmas I go to Spitalfields Market and buy the best oranges, apples, bananas, etc., which we put into poly-thene bags with half a pound of real butter and a quarter of tea. These are delivered on Christmas Eve. I get the biggest turkey money can buy, and a good ham, which the Red Ensign Club cook for us. On Christmas Day a band of willing helpers take round hot dinners, and someone calls again on Boxing Day to see if every-thing is all right. All this costs about £60, but we have generous gifts from Twining Crosfield and other firms.

I thought I might have difficulty in getting together a band of people to do the donkey work—and going up six or seven flights of steps with dinners is real work. But I have never had any trouble at all, and our own simple festivities have been enjoyed all the more.

A letter of thanks from one of these old ladies shows that the old warm-hearted Cockney spirit is still very much alive. She writes:

"Thank you for my lovely Christmas dinner—whoever cooked it was an Artist. I was so cheered by the charming young gentleman asking and offering me my taste in bottled beer—one hears so much about Christians (I avoid them whenever possible) but all you who gave so unselfishly to cook and tramp round to an old woman on *your* own Christmas Day and then that delightful human warm kindly touch (good old Beer) brought to my mind the real meaning of Christ and Christmas and *Christians* and I am still thinking about and will treasure the memory."

In an area like Stepney there is plenty to keep a parish priest busy. A woman with T.B., living at the top of Royal Albert Buildings, is ordered by the doctors to keep free of stairs and carrying things. Can I write to the housing authorities about getting her a bungalow? An ex-sailor with an evil-smelling cancer lives with his wife in a two-roomed flat in the Peabody Buildings. The shared lavatory and one tap are at the end of a long stretch of stone corridor. His wife cannot stand it much longer and is tempted to leave him. A father of five, one of my best families, indulges in "fiddling" like most of his friends, gets caught, and is sent to prison. His wife is afraid I will not want the children to come to church any more. A teenage son takes up with bad company. A daughter gets into trouble. Somebody must be got into hospital in a hurry. There is no resident doctor in the parish, although three doctors have practices and keep surgery hours.

This sort of practical kindness is the "shop floor" on which all theological students and young clergymen ought to be willing to work. If they cannot meet the people on this level they are not going to be much good. I and my staff have gone straight from an early Holy Communion service to carry coal, light the fire, sweep up and make tea for some old lady who is too old or ill to go down four flights of stairs to fetch coal for herself, and cannot afford to tip the coalman to carry it up. Mrs. Bull, blind and helpless at eighty, might have died of cold if I had not taken coal to her from my own store, then waited for her coalman and got him to take it upstairs.

I was delivering "The Pilot", the parish magazine, in a café in East Smithfield one day. The owner was ill with cancer of the face and his wife was slaving to keep the place going, though the customers, mostly dockers, helped all they could. The sink trough was piled up with dirty dinner and tea plates, and the poor woman was trying to cook the meals and serve them all by herself. My reputation bounded when I pulled off my cassock and dived into the dirty dishes, and kept at it until all was clear and clean. Things like this mean far more to most people than Church services, and I have received blessings from these helpless people far richer than any could receive from any Church authority.

But though I and my helpers were kept busy with routine parish work, I was never able to forget the special work to which I knew God was calling me.

It was over seven years ago when I realised that I must do something about the declining moral standards in my part of Stepney, and leave the more respectable part to look after itself, except for emergencies. Almost in a moment my eyes were opened to the changing situation in the parish and its surroundings. I felt that I was wasting my time in going to the doors of those who knew what they ought to be doing. They liked my visits, but did nothing about it. Besides, the Cable Street side of the parish was fast going downhill. Every shop that shut was bought up and opened as a café, and girls from all over the British Isles and Eire were flooding in.

Like most people, I had always felt that little could be done for prostitutes, and anyhow what could a man do about it, priest or no priest? But before I received, from one of these girls, the challenge that was to make all the difference to my outlook, I had met one or two others who apparently felt I was a little out of the ordinary. One came to me with a wonderful bouquet that a special boy friend had sent her. When my wife answered the door, she handed her the flowers, saying, "Give these to Father, it's me birthday and they are too good for me, tell him to put them in the church." I put them in the best vase and placed them by the Blessed Sacrament Chapel, and for some months the picture was the cover for "The Pilot", my parish magazine.

Then another girl, who was to die tragically, could never pass me in the street without speaking, even when she was with her clients, to their discomfort and never mine. She would greet me and ask a blessing, and never once did I fail to warn her in the most friendly way of her end. Audrey was carefree in a pathetic sort of way. She was thin, weak chested, yet always neat, and she wore her hair in a pony tail. I missed her for some time. Then I was visiting a woman in St. George's Hospital, Wapping, who pointed across the ward and said, "See that woman over there, Father, she's no good." I said, "Neither am I, Gill," but I did not look in the direction she indicated, and neither did I give her some toffees I had brought her. I moved on to the next bed, and the next. Then I looked in the direction given me, and there was Audrey. She met my eyes and I went over to her. It was obvious that she hadn't long to live, and she couldn't do what she was told by the doctors. I prayed with her and blessed her, and gave her the toffees. The poor girl discharged herself soon afterwards, and went on board one of the ships in the dock. On leaving, she slipped, fell into the dock and was drowned. Her friends talked to me about her, and one of them gave me a copy of the only snap ever taken of her, saying tearfully, "She was always generous and kind, and never rowed." For myself I never knew anyone who appreciated my friendship more than Audrey; her respect for me shamed me.

It was not long after this that Mary gave me my commission, and, as a journalist said, after I told her the story, "You nearly refused it." It was the beginning of Lent, 1955. I was making my way towards the vicarage through Cable Street, and was suddenly aware of someone swearing at me good and proper: "It's just because I am a bloody prostitute that you pass me by." It didn't disturb me a lot, because I don't pass people by intentionally. Anyhow, I stopped and said, "I am deaf in one ear, what is it?"

Mary came up to me and I shook her by the hand. I think I must have seen her as she had been when she was young and indeed beautiful, for she had dark hair and really lovely eyes and features. Then, before I realised it, she had just run away. I stood and wondered and then went slowly home. Half an hour later I came out with my wife and sister to take my midweek Lent Service, and outside the vicarage was Mary. She drew me aside: "I have brought you a present, Father." Like the rest of the Cable Street prostitutes, she was obviously near the gutter of poverty. As I felt I wanted to be on the side of the giving, I told her, "I don't want your present." Hardly had I got the words out when I got another well-dressed cursing. So I said, "Give me your present, what have you got for me?" It was a small box of chocolates, but the nature of the gift doesn't matter. What does matter is that in accepting Mary's present, I accepted my commission from God to do all I could for prostitutes for the rest of my days.

It is seven years since that happened, and I have been in touch with Mary ever since. I have helped her often and she has stayed at Church House two or three times. When she has been in hospital or in trouble, she has asked me to go and see her. Two years ago she was sent to Manchester prison for three years. It wasn't that she had committed a crime worthy of such a sentence, but the Recorder, considering her previous record of twenty-seven convictions, thought it wise to shut her up for a long period. I went to see her twice in Manchester prison, and wrote to the Home Secretary on her behalf. She was transferred to Holloway so that it would be easier for the only friends she had in the world to visit her.

Mary is now in Broadmoor, where we visit her and keep enough money at her disposal to buy her a daily paper and some cigarettes. I have quoted many of her letters to me, and put them into print. One thing she repeats over and over again—"If there had been places like Church House twenty years ago, I am sure I should not be where I am now." I believe her. The other thing she keeps repeating is, "I only have you in all the world." In that "you" must be included my lady colleagues at Church House, for we are all at one in our work.

CHAPTER II

Slums in Stepney

THE years before Church House opened were a particularly chaotic time for our part of Stepney. The property owners who stayed in the area had no trouble in letting so-called furnished rooms for very high rents, and they didn't much mind how the rooms were used. There were constant rumours of slum houses and derelict houses being pulled down. Because of this, landlords sold the property to Maltese, Greeks, Somalis, West Indians, West Africans, Cypriots and others. Property in Grace's Alley was sold in this way, and here was a particular scandal, for the property was fit only for complete demolition and I am quite sure it ought to have been condemned if it wasn't already. I found patching up and repairs going on during the night hours. I appealed both to the Local Authorities and the London County Council. I had photographs taken of the property at the back and the front. Still the work was allowed to go on. A café was gutted with fire yet the derelict property, in an area which should be completely demolished, has had a notice "For Sale" and the name of agents for over a year now.

My schools in Wellclose Square had low railings until four years ago. Over these railings lousy mattresses were dumped during the night hours. Women's toilet towels were thrown over, and french letters which teachers found the children blowing up with their mouths. Our excellent school keeper tried to collect and burn these things before the children's play time. I wrote several times to the London County Council, giving these crude facts, always with invitations to come down and see.

Opposite the property in Grace's Alley is a smallish but deep bomb site. This was used for years as a dump for every kind of filth from cafés. Slops of the foulest kind were poured into it until it stank to high heaven. Our school children were often found playing on that lot. For years I badgered every authority including the Medical Officer of Health. The Town Clerk wrote saying how difficult it was, and that the only remedy was to build a wall. The wall is now built, and the effect has been to make the concealed filth heap worse than before. The normal cleansing of our part of Stepney is a scandal. The Cleansing Officer has his office in this particular area, yet even in its immediate vicinity the rubbish dumps are never cleared. There is a foul dump site which is never touched right opposite the nice post office.

Then derelict buildings are broken into, if any force to enter is needed, by men and women who live rough in them. Many of these are methylated spirit drinkers who are particularly bad in every way. They are quite mad and irresponsible when under the influence of the stuff and very ill with hunger when they sober up. One youngish Scot who used to be a sailor has been a meth drinker for years. He curses me and has spat at me when drunk many times, but when sober he is near to death. On one occasion I met him, and because he was staggering, I took him to be drunk and made as if to avoid him. I only just heard him say, "Don't pass me, Father," and I realised he was ill. I took him to my baker's, a general store which sells milk, butter and cheese. As I got to the door, the shopkeeper cried, "Keep that man outside, Father, or we won't get the stench of him out of the shop today." He was not exaggerating. Most of the cafés, even of the lowest type, will not allow meth drinkers in. Their breath is like a bad sewer and, even more horrible, when in drink they cannot contain themselves. I kept my man outside and got milk, bread, butter, and cheese. I cut the bread in the shop and buttered it and got the cheese arranged, and took the lot outside. He whispered pathetically, "I can't sit anywhere, people won't let me." So I took him to my vicarage door which has three steps outside, and I sat him down with his food.

The police came to know that my steps were sanctuary. Two old ladies sit on them every day for about half an hour at midday, and people I feed and rest sit on a special side. An old humbug of a bum, known as the Admiral, once had an argument with a police officer who tried to turn him off the steps. When it came to the "laying on of hands", the Admiral suggested that the officer should ring my door bell. When I came out, I had to confirm the claim that my steps are sanctuary. The police are very kind, and I keep in with them, but they often think I am impossible.

So long as the derelict buildings are allowed to stand, we cannot hope to see any improvement in our general living conditions. Not only are the down-and-outs drawn to our area, seeking free shelter, but families who have lived in Stepney for years are finding themselves crowded into one or two rooms, and it is quite impossible for respectable newcomers to find decent lodgings.

In one day I received two letters, one from the Rev. George Appleton, then Rector of St. Botolph's, Aldgate, asking if I knew of any family who would take in a reformed prisoner with no place to live, and the other from a woman who wrote:

"Dear Father Joe,

"I read your article in the *News of the World* and I would like you also to listen to my story.

"I have six children all in a L.C.C. home, and I have only two rooms broken down, holes in the floor, and have been on the waiting list to be rehoused twelve years, my children have been away about three years. They are getting increasingly disturbed now I am told it's not a good idea to have them home at weekends because they are getting increasingly disturbed and are hard to handle when they get back. I have been ill since the children went away, and I am constantly worrying about them, especially my baby who is only $2\frac{1}{2}$.

"I have had my case in the *East End Advertiser*, but it has made no difference. My big boy ran away last week, after walking from Woolwich, and I had to take him back, he is twelve and he certainly is getting very disturbed.

"The L.C.C. says that my family is *too* big, and that I need a four bedroomed house, and so I have to keep on waiting. I am heartbroken, when I see people getting houses after arriving in this country of only a few months. I have done everything I could but it makes no difference, they state that my conditions, though bad, there are people that are in more urgent need. My husband is a good worker, and I have worked as a telephonist, but I cannot work any more because I have deteriorated in health. I read cases of people who don't want their children, and I am dying to have mine with me but cannot because of housing.

"We are fumigated every so often for bugs, and everywhere we have great big mouse holes, and we haven't any water upstairs. When my children come up at week-ends, they ask me why they have to go back, so now they don't come up any more, I have to go and visit and take two out at a time, and it seems awful that I have to take two, and leave four behind when they are all my children. Still, if you answer my letter you will be able to give me added strength to carry on, I know you must have the interest of Stepney at heart by what I have seen in the paper.

"Hoping you will write to me.

"Yours sincerely,
"MRS. G. M. SILAS."

Received 7th November 1961.

I sent a copy of Mrs. Silas' letter to the Minister of Housing, the Chairman of the London County Council Building Committee and others. It seems that the Ministry of Housing and the public authorities lack initiative and are afraid of laying down the law. Apart from a lot of needless over-building of fancy offices and flats, which could be curbed, there is much building that could surely be stopped altogether until our slumland is cleaned up and flats and houses built for the people who are crippled with frustration.

Everybody knows the attraction for all builders of nice offices in good areas, and there is no doubt that that is where the money is. I have been told that the architects who do this sort of work would not do the work we want done in Stepney. Perhaps if they had no other work for five or six years they would develop a taste for it. To turn horrors like our part of Stepney into something beautiful would be a truly great achievement. Rebuilding is not only desirable, in the interests of civic dignity; it is necessary on grounds of the most elementary humanity. Men, women and children should not be expected to go on living in conditions like this.

How much longer is it to be allowed to go on? I have been sticking my neck out about it for ten years, and I have had to fight for every small concession. I am glad to say that Mrs. Silas has now been promised accommodation and put on the top of the housing list.

As recently as February 1962 I visited two houses in Cable Street. In one there were two families of five each living in two small rooms, one for each family. They had been given notice to quit because the place was falling in on them. One room was exposed to the heavens, and the heavy snow which was falling was coming in. A wall of the other room had caved in. These people had nowhere else to go. Further down the street, a couple with eight children and two others in hospital were living in one frightful room. It was furnished, so-called, so the landlord had the power to put them out at any time.

What have these people done to deserve such terrible conditions? People who know no better sometimes write off slum-dwellers as shiftless lay-abouts, squandering the pay packet on drink, and deserving nothing better than a slum to live in. But these are good, hard-working families, normal cheerful East enders who haven't changed much since the days of my boyhood. They mostly work in the docks or in local factories, while many of the girls go off to office jobs in the City. Such decent people do not particularly want to move away from their relations and friends, but there is no hope of suitable rehousing in Stepney, so those who can are moving out of the area, while more and more of the worst kind of outsiders are moving in. I was greeted in Cable Street one morning by a man who with his family had moved from a filthy building in Grace's Alley to another part of London. He stopped to thank me for helping him to get the house. "We're right next door to the gas-works, but it's like living in the country after all this," he told me, looking round him.

The situation has been made far worse by the numbers of im-migrants from overseas who have moved into the area. On the very day that I received Mrs. Silas' letter, there were ten West Indians

in Cable Street going from door to door looking for accommodation.

Now I do not doubt for a second the deep sincerity of those whose
gospel is, "Let-em-all-come", and I want to make it clear that they
do not love their overseas brothers more than I do. But the position
is now chaotic. Before the passing of the Immigration Act, bad
characters as well as good were flooding in in their thousands, and
while the good settled down and found themselves jobs, there were
a great many who lived for a while on public assistance and then
started to look for easy money in all sorts of rackets.

Many of them have bought up houses which they let out room
by room at high rents to unsuspecting new immigrants, who find
themselves living in conditions which would be condemned for
stock on a farm. And while I do not want to lay the blame for our
terrible conditions in Stepney altogether on people from overseas,
it is a fact that most of the bad cafés and clubs that have been
opened in the area over the past few years are owned by Maltese,
Somalis, Cypriots, West Indians, and other immigrants. Newcomers tend to look for people of their own country, and so they
come crowding into Stepney, many of them poor, ignorant, sick
and weak-minded people who, not knowing where to turn, are
exploited by their own fellow-countrymen. East Londoners are
normally a cheerful and friendly people, but can we wonder that
they are becoming embittered when they see their living accommodation taken up by newcomers, and their homes being turned
into slums? And I wonder what the officials of the Health Department were thinking of when they questioned our most sanitary
conditions in Church House, while not a stone's throw away there
are cafés in filthy surroundings with dirty living conditions, amid
which food is allowed to be cooked and fed to people night and day?
These are things that should concern us all. Every priest and
parson, every bishop, archbishop or cardinal should condemn the
mess.

This problem of immigration seems to frighten a lot of people,
politicians and Church leaders. Very great care must be taken that
restrictions shall not be interpreted as prejudice of any kind. Yet
it would be a mistake to continue to allow more and more people

into the country while our own people are desperate for living accommodation.

The brothers of the Anglican Society of St. Francis, who until recently had a house at 84 Cable Street, did a great deal to help the coloured people in Stepney, among them many who were mentally and physically ill. Soon after I came to Stepney, Father Neville, with three other brothers, came to ask if I had any accommodation for his evening school for coloured men. So for nearly seven years, three nights a week, our basement was full of our Commonwealth brothers, with one white person to teach one coloured. It was busiest during the winter months, and our greatest difficulty was to get teachers as well as students to shut the door after them. Since this school began, I have been very conscious of the lack of knowledgeable and educated coloured men to teach their own people. White people could be had, but never a coloured student, in spite of the large number of coloured students in London. This has led me to the belief that something just as bad as the "colour bar" is afoot, in the "class bar" between the coloured people themselves.

When the possibility of trouble between the bad elements of Black and White became apparent at the time of the Notting Hill riots, the coloured people were in a state of terror; they had no coloured shepherd to guide them, and they would not trust a white man. An educated coloured man who had a post at the L.C.C. came to my vicarage with another man to ask for a hall for their people to meet in. I at once offered my church. But I emphasised the wisdom of notifying the police of any meetings. They did not agree, and went away. I was very disturbed, and consulted Father Charles of the Franciscans. Often distrust of one's fellow men can extend to dangerous lying, and here was a case in point. I had offered them my church so that they could be safe and free from interruption, but Father Charles overheard one of them saying, "We asked Father Williamson to lend us his church, and he would not." He broke in on this conversation, and told them he knew I had assured them the church was available. Sadly, as a result of their fear, the coloured community seemed to hate us all.

I walked the streets for three nights until very late. I warned the police of the meeting, so that protection could be arranged for the great numbers of coloured people who were coming from all parts. Before I discovered where the meeting was to be held, a poor mentally-deficient man followed me round shouting, and might have struck me had it not been for some of his own people holding him back. On the night of the meeting the police were out in strength, and I did not want the man run in, although it might have been better for him to be in the safety of a cell. Then, against the advice of the Police Superintendent, I went into the overcrowded workshop off Cable Street where the meeting was to take place. I wanted to get to the leaders and to assure them of my help and advise them to break up quickly. I went up the rough wooden steps to the room, and tried to make myself heard, but I was told to go by terrified, grey, wide-eyed people. I felt sick and sad that they would not trust me.

Going back through Cable Street, I saw three of our own determined white thugs. I walked slowly behind them, and there was a very dangerous moment when my coloured shadow appeared and began to shout abuse at me. But he was sane enough to see his danger, and fled as the lads looked at him. I pleaded with the boys to keep the peace. They did not answer me, but went away out of the street.

The following Sunday the coloured people had another meeting, in the church hall of St. George's-in-the-East, at which a coloured Doctor of Law was among the speakers and a friend of mine from the L.C.C. presided. It was not a nice meeting, but the Chairman stressed the importance of coloured people trying to live like the white man when they settled in his country. He was candid about the all-night parties, the blaring music and the drunkenness which caused so much unrest. It was sad listening to one speaker who lived by evil business and was more responsible than most for the trouble. His talk was sheer humbug.

At the meeting the intellectuals who presided agreed to keep in touch with their poorer and more ignorant brothers, and coloured people living in Stepney resolved to have regular meetings and to cope with the bad elements among themselves. There were in fact no race riots in Stepney, but the promises were forgotten and conditions have grown steadily worse. A very large area of the borough is noisy and very, very horrible. I am convinced that bad immigrants from the Commonwealth should be deported like those from foreign countries. The bad name they get for their own people by their evil lawless behaviour makes it very much harder for the decent, hardworking men and women from overseas to earn an honest living. It is doubly bad for our coloured friends who were born here or have been here for very many years.

The Franciscan brothers had a hostel and club in their Cable Street premises, for friendless coloured men. Their policy was changed according to circumstances. At first their little hostel was for men who had no place to live and wanted shelter and food while working. Then there was a time when many of the men were weak-minded and little could be done for them. One winter there was a particularly wretched man, a mental case, who would creep into the hostel to get warm. But often he stood or sat in the bitterly cold street. He could move very little, and would just stay and shiver. When he did get into the club he would sit over the fire, and often nearly fall into it as he dozed. On one occasion another man, also mentally ill, sat on the other side of the fire. Their heads must have touched as they dozed, or they might have thought the other was getting too much of the fire. Like two wild animals they flew at each other, while the other men who were there singing and playing billiards roared with laughter and cheered them on. The brothers eventually stopped the fight.

These were two of the many unfortunate immigrants who were either mentally sub-normal when they came, or have become so through their failure to stand up to English conditions. Again and again the good brothers got them into hospitals as voluntary patients, and again and again the poor men would discharge themselves.

So Stepney and places like it become reception centres for the weak, the mentally deficient, the unemployable, and the bad. Such people are drawn here because there are derelict houses into which they can creep when they have little or no money. They live in these filthy places after a fashion, eating what scraps they can scrounge.

CHAPTER III

Worsening Conditions

As time went by, it was obvious that conditions were steadily getting worse. It was not just the overcrowding and the slums. Stepney was rapidly becoming a centre for all kinds of vice. More and more cafés and clubs were opening for the convenience of prostitution and dope-peddling, and clients were coming in from all parts of London.

On one of my visits to a pub to sell my magazine, I was invited by a sailor to "come and meet the girls". I sat in that bar in my cassock and biretta with four girls and they were from Scotland, Ireland, Wales and the North of England, and they had been brought to Stepney by lorry drivers. I didn't preach to them, but we spoke of the kind of life they were living. They were nice girls and they hated the life. They had all been dumped without a penny and there was no place for them to stay. They had come for normal work. The lorry drivers had given them lifts, and fed them on the journey to London, and had had their "fun" in return; then, being married men, they were anxious to get rid of them—the sooner the better. Penniless and without shelter, the girls were easy prey for the café owners.

Naturally, my determination to fight this evil did not go down very well with the men who were working the vice rackets. I was never quite sure when I walked through the streets what was going to happen to me.

It came as a little surprise when an honest tough said to me: "You've gota lota friends, Faver." I had had a feeling of getting it in the neck from all quarters and had felt that those who might be friendly were afraid of exposing themselves. Many people endure the vice and noise because they are in deadly fear of what will happen if they complain.

A woman telephoned me and asked me to go to the place where she and her family lived. Overnight it had been changed from a normal East End residential quarter, where men and women went to work and went to bed at reasonable times, into a vice spot, where noise and horror reigned all night. A man who lived on club and café life had bought one house in the street, which made all the normal East Enders crave to be out of it. The cursing and vicious threats made the women afraid of being bashed up and their homes broken into. Because of this I was asked to go to the house after dark, or not to go in my cassock and biretta. The threat of violence is never far from day-to-day scenes.

So it was that in broad daylight I was cursed and threatened as I walked through Cable Street. I walked slower and slower to show face against this particularly vicious man. I felt I was going to be hit on the head and let myself go passive as I dawdled. There was a sudden scream of pain as the raised arm was gripped by one of the toughest and crudest men in the area, who growled: "Let 'im alone." I glanced back and saw the arm of my would-be assailant limp, and the man in pain as he waited for his arm to come back to normal

Again, my doorbell was pressed and pressed after 10.30 one Saturday night. I went to the door and found three men waiting, and I knew at once they had come to beat me up. I deliberately went out amongst them and shut the door behind me. They spat and cursed to give themselves courage to do the deed, yet somehow they could not touch me, although they wanted to, and after some minutes they went away. Going into church the next morning a neighbour called to me and he said: "You had some beauties round you last night, Vicar." I replied: "I didn't notice you about." "No, you didn't," he said, "and you didn't see two of the best dockers with me, we would 'ave killed the . . . if they had touched you." It made me feel the comfort of friends, but I thought I had strange guardian angels. The parish priest in Stepney has to learn to be fearless as well as loving.

Some of us who were concerned about the downward trend of

the area decided to meet together to discuss what we could do about it.

A small committee was formed, consisting of the Rural Dean, the Franciscan Fathers and myself, together with Miss Edith Ramsay and Miss Margaret Paterson, who was at that time the Probation Officer of Thames Police Court. It was a simple and rather rough sort of meeting. Out of it came a pamphlet, "Vice Increase in Stepney". Although it was written by Edith Ramsay, it bore all our names as we thought this would help to strengthen the cause. I got it printed, and some 5,000 copies were sent to Members of Parliament, lords, bishops and all organisations interested. That pamphlet marked the beginning of the very hard road to get the Government, the Opposition, the Churches and the people to realise the dangers we were running into, not only in Stepney, but in very many other areas.

A summary of "Vice Increase in Stepney", written in 1957, makes interesting reading in 1962. It gives the Home Office statistics for England and Wales for prosecution for soliciting. For the years 1930-34 the average was 1,555. In 1955 the figure had risen to 11,926. Statistics for soliciting in Stepney show the moral decline. There were two prosecutions in 1946; nine in 1949; 585 in 1956.

The pamphlet told a pretty horrifying story. It contrasted pre-war Stepney—poor and badly housed, but with high moral standards—with the picture of open vice in 1956. The Aldgate end of Commercial Road was notorious for its "street waitresses", standing about singly or in groups waiting to attract men, and trade in a near-by alley or doorway. Flats and rooms in semi-derelict buildings were sub-let at fantastic rents for this degrading traffic. Other forms of indecency, including male prostitution, were not uncommon.

A local resident wrote, about this time: "It is becoming impossible for our wives to go out after dark without being accosted by men who hang around outside; also a number of prostitutes who have no rooms here are taking their clients into our passages and yards and leaving behind filth of every description. There is a number of very small children here who have to play somewhere, and I think it a disgrace that they see things like this. It's time something was done. The police do their best, and nightly search passages and yards; but it doesn't stop them, as they are back again as soon as the police go away."

Few of these girls are Londoners, and fewer still come from Stepney. A lot of them have spent their early years in homes and institutions. They are the idle, the homeless, the rejects of stable society, and in the community of vice they find a sort of fellowship they cannot find in other social groupings. There is a security in "belonging" to the men who organise the traffic, and they can be sure of a roof over their heads.

Empty houses for sale were promptly bought up by pimps, and filled with their women. It is difficult enough to preserve the decencies of life in condemned buildings, where one lavatory serves three families. Stepney, in the past, was familiar with those difficulties, but now there was the added horror of an increasing number of these flats being let to prostitutes, while queues of men waited their turn outside. "I can't let my boy visit me here now," said one woman of her son who was working away from London. But there were many families with children in the flats. From their earliest years they took prostitution for granted. The innocence of childhood could never be theirs.

All this we put into our report which was published a few months before the Wolfenden Committee reported. The Street Offences Act which followed, has reduced the activities of prostitutes in the open, but the general climate of the area is very much the same five years later. We have even become a show piece for sightseers. Teenagers come from other parts of the East End and parade Cable Street in groups to watch the "fun". I was showing a City official round when a dozen strange, very young girls, appeared in one of our worst streets. When I expressed surprise, he replied, "Don't you realise it's the beginning of the school holidays?" One day a coach load of students from the Continent pulled into Ensign Street; their American guide led them into a café-club, and shouted, "You'll find everything here"—and indeed they would: prostitution, drugs, gambling—the lot. These slum clubs are the deal setting for underground life of the most vicious kind, yet the

L.C.C., who urged me to help prevent a particular club opening, a year later informed me that they and the police were allowing a licence for two years.

The police are always raiding these places, but it seems to make little difference to business. After a break of a few hours, they are full again. The policewomen take an important part in these raids when prostitutes are about. The van into which the girls are escorted or carried is known locally as the "meat van". The "meat van" is always at work, but it took me a long time to comprehend the significance of the name.

With all this we had everything going on in the streets, and the police quite unable to cope with the incidents for their frequency. Because of the increase in prostitution in the area, and because it was taken so much for granted and little could be done, it became quite unsafe for decent young girls to go about the place. One of my girls whom I was preparing for Confirmation used to come to the vicarage soon after she left her work. One evening when she was due I heard a bump and crash against the door and I hurried out to find her in an almost collapsed condition. She had been followed and pestered by two Maltese. It had happened before, but she had been too sensitive to tell me. I took up the telephone and spoke to the Superintendent of the Police, and I wrote directly to the Prime Minister. But to the men, who would very quickly be run in for pestering girls in their own country, it was child's play here, where any girl at any time could be treated as a potential prostitute, the police being few and far between.

One of the troubles in Stepney is that there are just not enough policemen, and when they are needed they are often engaged elsewhere. There are hours when a policeman cannot be seen. I have had leading authorities of the L.C.C. and M.P.s remark to me at the end of a tour that they have not seen a single one. Often, really often, there can be the most horrible fights between women, or men bashing and kicking their women about, and it can be half an hour or more before the police arrive.

An area like Cable Street at the west end of it should never be left without supervision, and reliefs should take the place of those busy with arrests. Police cars and vans are necessary, but the man on the beat is the real power; the sight of him makes people much more reasonable, even in drink. Perhaps the greatest scandal was when three men in the open committed sodomy in Wellclose Square. That could not happen if foot patrolling were regular. The Police Superintendent was kind enough to meet me with the local people the night afterwards, and police dogs were introduced, but the night Superintendent said it couldn't happen because he had been round the Square in his car. I have seen the police car going round that square, and they would miss everything and anything going on if the people stood still. The car is gone as soon as it arrives.

I myself have seen public indecency going on in the open streets. One evening as I was escorting a lady guest back to Aldgate East tube station at 11 p.m., we saw a crowd of men outside a public house. In the centre of the ring was a young woman dancing with abandon, wearing nothing but shoes and stockings and a thin frock which she held high as she danced. Another light summer evening I came through Grace's Alley into Ensign Street on my way home, and there I found a group of my school children with a lot of coloured men watching a man and a prostitute having sexual intercourse.

I do not write these things out of a wish to be sensational. I write them because people should know that these things can happen in London, on the very doorstep of the City of which our town planners are so proud. I write them because these people are our brothers and sisters, and because young children are growing up in places where they can see this kind of thing going on every day, even though the Street Offences Act has driven them partly underground. We close our eyes to these evils and say, "It doesn't concern me," or, "If people choose to behave in this way, what right have we to stop them?" But we share their guilt unless we fight the evil conditions in which such vice flourishes. Failing that, we shall soon have the most wonderfully regulated, spotless city, with well-built skyscrapers of office blocks, while less than half a mile away there are the worst slums imaginable.

There is no doubt that the children are among the greatest

K

sufferers from these conditions. Respectable parents cannot hope to keep them from dreadful sights, and others do not try. In 1955, in a letter to *The Times*, I wrote that there is something far worse than a brothel, and that is being a prostitute's children watching mother work. I received letters from all sorts of knowledgeable people telling me all sorts of things about brothels which it was supposed I did not know. One noble Lord did not spare his words in condemning me. A gracious old lady told me she knew all about Stepney, for she had been through it and stopped her coach many times to speak to the people. Poor dears, but had any of them been close enough to prostitution to have known, as I had, really intelligent children of a prostitute living in the atmosphere of mother's trade? My noble Lord did not answer my letter about that, and I suspect he felt that such things could not happen here in England, and that I might be a liar!

Opinions and policies are divided among Child Welfare authorities about the importance of keeping children with their mothers. It is said that it is better for children to live with a bad woman who is their mother than to be put into care. Circumstances vary. I have seen a mother start her daughter into prostitution. I stopped them in the street and told them what I thought, solemnly and severely. The mother's only reply was, "You can't stop her now, she is seventeen." I could never have believed it if I hadn't seen it, and if I hadn't known both mother and daughter very well indeed. In two years that girl looked like a woman of thirty-five and haggard at that. That sort of life makes old women from young girls in a short time.

How hopeless I felt as I thought about these girls. How impossible it seemed for a priest to try to help them without women colleagues. Yet during the three years when I was trying to get a woman worker, I was able to help many. As I left the Franciscan chapel one day after Mass, I found a group of men at the door of a nearby café. Their eyes were glued to a spot opposite and I found myself looking in that direction. A poor girl of only sixteen was trying to offer herself for food. It was just that. You could read it in her eyes, yet her condition was such that men could only look at her and leave her; she was the most pathetic sight possible.

I went across and spoke to her. She had two pennies in her hand. "I will go to work if you will help me," she said. I did all I could for her. I gave her money and an address to go to. The men who looked on were a tough lot, but they looked their gratitude. A good deed is rarely forgotten, and it is spoken about afterwards. Incidents like this made me all the more determined to go on with my project for opening a hostel for these girls.

CHAPTER IV

The Founding of
Church House

IT was something of a miracle that Church House was started at all. The W.V.S. and the Y.W.C.A., with a few of us, had long felt the very great need of a girls' hostel in Stepney. But in Stepney itself very few indeed were interested in the venture. Not only so, there seemed to be bitter opposition where there should have been helpful leadership.

The W.V.S. called a meeting which the Town Clerk promised to attend. He did not come. We telephoned him and he apologised, but he had some important work on hand. Without official action of some sort, little or nothing could be done. Nothing official ever has been done since. Other efforts were made to come to the rescue of stranded girls, but nothing was achieved, so most of them found themselves in the hands of the only people who would help them, and that for their own gain: the men who opened the cafés for the absolute convenience of prostitution.

Those of us who loved East London and watched this happening could get no help to stop it. I brought the matter up many times at our Rural Deanery meetings. I told them that I had counted twenty-three prostitutes in two small bars of one pub, and had gone from there only 100 yards into Cable Street and counted up to a hundred. They did not believe me, and I was accused of exaggeration. I wrote to Joost de Blank, then our bishop. He was kind, but he told me to "Keep my powder dry and I would go to town in a big way." As a priest-friend said, "What you want is more powder." Even my motive in fighting our terrible conditions was questioned; for an old and influential priest of standing told me before a large gathering, "If you go on like this, you will be made a Prebendary."

This general opposition did not deter me in the slightest, for I was sure I was meant to go on. To bring the matter more before the public eye, I wrote to the Dean of St. Paul's asking him to allow me to preach in the Cathedral. Bishop Wand replied that there would not be a vacancy for a very, very long time, and asked if I would like the Cathedral to pray for my work. I then wrote to the Dean of Westminster, who sent me a donation, but ignored my request. Had either of these gentlemen allowed me to preach it would have been terribly tough stuff, and I would, of course, have handed my material to the Press and so given it the widest publicity.

But the kind of publicity I wanted was not to come that way, and much more work had to be done. I had to see my first lady church worker almost knocked out with fatigue in the first few weeks of her work in the parish.

Nora Neal came to me in September 1957. She had been working in Hackney, but for thirteen years, including the war years, she had worked in this area and was just the person I needed to tackle the work which I, as a man, could not begin to do amongst women and girls. She was kept busy from the start. Hardly had she settled into her lodgings in Mrs. Maaser's house in Wellclose Square when her bed and sofa were occupied by girls in distress, and she herself was kindly given a share of Mrs. Maaser's bed.

The first girl she was able to help was a young married woman who had come down from the north. Miss Paterson, the Probation Officer, telephoned me to say that she had had a communication from the north asking for her help. A young mother had been enticed away from her home by a Maltese, and had left her husband and two small children. The husband had found a piece of paper with an address on it, a number in Cable Street. He said he did not mind what his wife had done, he would forgive her, he loved her, and above all he wanted her back with the children. I got Nora on the track.

A girl Nora knew was behind the counter in the café, so conversation was easy. Was Rhoda there? There was a girl who was with a Maltese living downstairs but she wasn't in. She was usually in about 6 o'clock.

Nora missed her that day, and hung about the next day. When Rhoda put in an appearance, Nora asked if she were from a certain place. She was. Could they have a talk? Yes, but Nora must come downstairs.

They went down. A room about 9 feet square had been made into two with match boarding. The half they entered had three bunks in it, and on each bunk there lay a half-dressed Maltese. Through the match-boarding door there was no room except for one small bed. There was no other furniture. They sat on the bed and talked.

Rhoda was very depressed. She said she hadn't thought it was going to be like this, and decided she would go back home. Nora tried to get her to leave then, but poor Rhoda said she couldn't do that, she must wait and tell Chrispin. Nora left her a card with her address.

Chrispin came in at 10 o'clock, and when Rhoda told him of her decision, though it was raining and it was late, he kicked her into the street and flung her bag after her. She went to Nora, and Nora put her into her own bed. Next day we took her to the station, and sent off a wire. At Christmas we exchanged cards, toys were sent to the babies, and I wrote to the husband. That was one story that ended happily.

It was about this time that I went to a Moral Welfare meeting, where we discussed prostitution and girls in moral danger, and their need for care. I said then that I was going to open a house for them, and I am quite sure the others thought I was mad. On my way back from that meeting I met the man who with his wife and child lived in part of Church House. He said, "You will be glad to know that I have got a place in the country." I was indeed glad, for here was my only hope of a house, and it is part of my freehold.

News soon gets around. When the family who rented the up-stairs part of the house heard that I was going to take in prosti-tutes, the husband really took me to town on the issue, and the more I tried to assure him that I could not do such a thing until he and his family were out of the building, the more he disbelieved me. The upshot was that he left Church House in a fortnight. So the house was free and mine to do what I liked with.

I hadn't a penny, and the place was in a very bad state of repair. Great alterations had to be made. A few good friends knew of my hopes and plans, among them Mr. A. G. Nesbitt, one of the London Diocesan architects. He suggested that the City Parochial Charities might help me with my scheme. I wrote to Sir Donald Allen at once and he gave me an appointment. I poured out my soul to him, and I didn't think I had got anywhere, but his Committee of Trustees voted me £1,000 for repairs and alterations. Their payments were made directly to the builders at my own request. The £1,000 was spent, and £800 besides.

A few months later, John Trevissic, of the *Church Times*, telephoned me and asked how things were going with our venture. I told him, and also told him of our debt of £800 .The upshot was that the *Church Times* wrote up our work, and in ten days I had received over £1,000.

It was at this time, too, that Mr. J. L. Reeves, the Managing Director of Colonial and Eagle Wharfs, gave me £100 on behalf of his fellow-directors. I told him I was £800 in debt, and that when the debt was paid off, I should want a treasurer. He at once offered to take on the job, and has in fact run all the business side of the Wellclose Square Fund ever since. There is not a busier man in the City of London, yet he willingly gives his time and talents to this work. It was Jim Reeves who organised the work on a business footing, and got together the Wellclose Square Committee.

The Committee has as its President the Bishop of Stepney; George Appleton, at that time Rector of the neighbouring St. Botolph's, Aldgate and now Archdeacon of London, is Chairman. Most denominations are represented. Edith Ramsay is a Presbyterian. She has battled in Stepney for its good for forty years and no one has been more courageous and helpful to me in my work. On the Committee too we have representatives of that grand Roman Catholic "Legion of Mary", and we are happy to help them by taking in Roman Catholic girls, though, like the old East

London pawnshop, "We take in anything." Our only object in our work is to make an escape for prostitutes and girls in moral danger, and to convert them to a normal way of life.

The new Bishop of Stepney, Evered Lunt, gave our work his full support from the start. When he came to address the Deanery clergy, soon afterwards, Father Neville raised the subject of the increase of prostitution in our area. I had kept my mouth shut on the subject at these meetings for some time, having been accused by some of my fellow clergy of exaggerating. So when the Rural Dean asked me if I had anything to say about it, I just shrugged my shoulders and said, a little naughtily, "You know what I think." The Bishop wasn't having that, and he asked me directly about conditions and if the cafés remained open all night. I replied, "Of course they do. All of them have notices on their doors to that effect, and the reason they stay open is to abet prostitution."

It was only a few weeks after this that the Bishop came to my vicarage. I had suspected that he had been told that I was over-drawing the picture of evil in our parish. His first words to me were: "I want to tell you that you do not exaggerate the conditions in this area. It is shocking; far worse than I expected." The good man had covered up his clerical collar and walked the streets through the night hours and the early morning, had himself been accosted several times, and had observed all the horrors that go on in the cafés and in the streets. He assured me of his backing, of his prayers, and his readiness to do anything he could to help.

All this time the work was growing, and by 1958 it was becoming very obvious that we should have to have another lady worker to help Nora Neal. I wrote to Daphne Jones, who was a Church worker at All Saints, Poplar and who had been there for twelve years. As a trained nurse she had worked in East London for eight years before that. It was she, in fact, who had put me in touch with Nora in the first place. Her rector, John Eastaugh, agreed to lend her to me for a year, but he was kind enough to say that he knew he would not see her again. Daphne came to us in June 1958, and has stayed ever since. She and Nora have made

Church House their home, and no less than 250 girls have been given hospitality and care.

The house was opened, without any fuss, in the summer of 1958. The formal Dedication, by the Bishop of Stepney, took place with full ceremony on 15th December, when every room was visited and blessed with prayer and incense. We wanted it to be a real home, without the hostel atmosphere of bare walls and imposed discipline of the convents which are in fact still, to their great credit, almost the only way of escape for girls on the streets. Up to six girls can live there at any one time, in single or shared bedrooms, where they can have their own things around them. There is a nice sitting-room with a television set, and they all eat together in the large kitchen. There are few rules, and those there are, are made to suit the comfort of everyone. We try to set a time for coming in at night, or the staff would find themselves being woken up at all hours. But otherwise the girls are free to come and go as they like, with no questions asked. Often they come to us in an exhausted condition, and to begin with they want to sleep, sleep, sleep, scarcely bothering about eating. Later we encourage them to find jobs and try to get them back to a normal sort of life. They may stay with us for a few weeks only, or for several months.

Our greatest difficulty is not to make it too easy for them to go on with prostitution or to go back to it. Before we had the second house, out of London, every time they went out to the cinema, or to buy cigarettes, or even to go to work they were faced with their old clients and with the cafés. The pull was too great for them. So what has happened is that we have rested them, cleaned them up, clothed them, got them back on their feet, and then they have walked out. Some have been clever enough to carry on the old café life and live at Church House at the same time. Several have stayed with us for a long time and then gradually gone back into bad ways. Even then they want to continue at Church House, but we have to tell them, "You must make the choice." They think us cruel for telling them to go, and it is terribly hard.

Others think we are locking them up, and have called Church House a prison, although any house less like a prison would be hard to find. On those occasions, I have gone to the door and opened it and told them their life is their own and they can go any time. Generally, though, we are deeply appreciated, and those who have left us are our friends for ever, and of course many of the girls have come back to us again and again, pleading to be let in for another try, and they nearly always get it.

But there have been a few who, for everyone's sake, we have had to refuse to allow back. We had two girls in particular who were in a bad state when they came in, and then, having gained strength and self assurance, they began, as so many of them do, to get back into the cafés. Added to that, they were lazy and wouldn't get up in the mornings. One or two trouble makers can upset all the rest. Nora did all she could, but was only sworn at. We hadn't had anything quite like this before. Nora telephoned me, and I went round at once. I stood outside their bedroom doors and called out that I would give them ten minutes to be up and out of the house before I called the police. Before they left, I had a talk with them and pulled no punches in telling them what they owed to Nora.

Next morning they turned up at the vicarage and apologised for their behaviour. I had to be hard-hearted and told them I hoped they hadn't said that just in the hope of coming back, because we couldn't have them. They accepted this, but asked if I could possibly fix them up somewhere else. I promised to help all I could, and phoned the usual hostels, only to find that the girls had stayed there before, and were on the black list; nobody would have them back. All I could do was to give them material help and guide them to a Reception Centre.

Neighbours criticise us, sometimes justly, when they see our girls behaving badly. But how little we realise what a hold their way of life has on them. Ordinary people may find it incredible that these women and girls do not seize any chance to get away from their sordid existence, but many of them have said to me: "You don't know what you are asking." The heavy smoker knows how hard and painful it is to escape from the habit. Drinking, dancing, gambling, among other attractions, can bind one body and soul. Think of your own strongest addiction and you will begin to understand the girl on the streets. There is, though, one great difference. Unless she goes right away from all her friends and associates, she can never escape from what she is, and to make a complete break with the present for an unknown and probably lonely future is too much for many girls.

Judy, who later came to us, wrote to me after seeing an article about our work in the *Empire News*: "I hate the life—it seems to create a very strong barrier between myself and the everyday decent people of this world. Believe me if I could get away from it all, I would do so like a flash—but as I have not known or been trained for any other kind of life—it has been very difficult for me to know where, or to whom, to turn . . . Keeping in mind (how could I ever forget) the fact that I am a prostitute, it is my strong belief that a house of hope and rehabilitation is the only answer to prostitution and the Street Offences Act . . . Just a decent clean room to call one's own, and to get a job and so hold one's head high in this unchristian, so lonely world."

This is, quite simply, what we are offering. Of course, we have to be prepared for all sorts.

It was Christmas 1959 when June, a weak-minded girl, who had only just left us, not so much because she was after men, as because she was weak and childish, was standing in Aldgate when Pat asked her for a light off her dog-end. Pat was hungry and desperate for shelter. June brought her to Church House, and there has hardly been a day since that her name has not been on the lips of one or other of us. We kept her for a long time and got her work, and there was a tremendous improvement in her all round. But she was a schizophrenic and we have had some very bad times with her. I believe that she (and those like her) should be kept in enforced care where she could work and earn her keep. Instead of which, although the poor girl had a long history of every kind of trouble and consequent restraint and punishment, she could go into a mental hospital only as a voluntary patient.

The great weakness of the Voluntary Patient Scheme is that the patients can walk out at any time, even when they are half doped. It seems to me that the system is unfair to the patient and, I should think, most unsatisfactory to the doctors. Why not make the term of the stay at least a month, or as long as the doctors feel an improvement can be made? I could have got Pat to sign for a month or more, and with the assurance of regular visits could have kept her steady. Sad to relate she has now landed in Broadmoor and, as she says, she doesn't know if it is "for the Queen's pleasure". But she is better there than being a menace to others, and a terrible responsibility to us at Church House.

She first began to play up when she led four others out late at night, to return in the early hours from the cafés. The fire escape was easy, but they had to climb like monkeys over a nine-foot wire fence guard, which they all did, returning the same way. Nora would have remained in ignorance had not Pat, in order to become the centre of attention, told her about it the next morning. We at once fixed up an electric bell to the fire escape door, whereupon Pat told us how to dismantle it or to turn it off.

She could be the kindest person possible, but she would say and do the foulest things to gain attention. She could not bear to be laughed at, and the girls are not always kind to each other. Because of this we nearly had a tragedy. We had warned another silly girl about tantalising Pat, but the girl persisted and sure enough Pat got her hands locked round her tormentor's neck. Mercifully, we had a very strong voluntary helper with us, and it was again fortunate that Nora Neal was in at the time. It took all their united strength to get Pat's hands unlocked, and then it was only by hurting her. They phoned for me, and when I arrived Pat was like death. I stayed with her until we could get her away. The whole staff knew that our work was being hampered by everything becoming centred round this one girl. We tried getting her a room outside and just giving her her meals at the Home, but she sat in Church House kitchen all day long.

We have been able to give some help to Pat and girls like her, but it just isn't enough to leave them to chance voluntary aid. Think of what is going on up and down the country where such girls, and indeed men, are left to run wild. I have been in touch with the Minister of Health and L.C.C. authorities about this matter but they are slow to move. Local clinics have been set up in some places. Stepney hasn't a centre yet. We got Pat linked up with a doctor, but when she refused treatment and walked out, he could do no more.

I brought up the case of Pat and that of others like her at a meeting of local clergy attended by the Superintendent and Chaplain of Long Grove Hospital. The general opinion was that if a patient discharged herself, that was the end of the matter. Is it the end of the matter, when people cannot control themselves and are allowed to roam wild? Are the general public expected to look after them? Is it sufficient for our wonderful Welfare State to allow girls who are mentally defective to be exploited as prostitutes?

Gloria is another schizophrenic, but she is easy going and in a sense subject to anyone who controls her at the moment. In her sane moments she is an interesting person. She came to us in a bad way but soon improved with a little kindness and help. She had been pushed around ever since she was young, and quite early in life became a prostitute with two children in care. She wanted to go straight, and left the man she was living with. I was talking to her in church one day, about getting strength through prayer. To emphasise what I was saying, I took her hand for a moment: "You can do it, you know," I urged her. It wasn't like talking to a person who knew nothing about prayer, for she had some ideas about it. But when she joined Nora later she took her on one side: "'Ere, is 'e all right?" When Nora asked why, she said, doubtfully: "Well, he held my hand, and the men do that."

Nora was horrified. She came to me almost in tears, begging me to be careful. Supposing someone should try to blackmail me! There is, of course, really no danger for if the attempt were made I should go straight to the Bishop, and then to the police. I like to tell this story in most of my talks, and it invariably brings an uncomfortable chuckle, which I soon cut short by saying, "The only touch that prostitutes know is an evil one."

On that first occasion when Mary met me in Cable Street, I shook hands with her and she ran away. She has told me over and over again that it was a shock to be greeted kindly and as an ordinary human being.

How many stories I could write about these girls! But even as I write, I am very conscious of the fact that these are not just "cases", but individual people, and my friends, and that even in writing of them under disguised names, I am in some sense betraying their confidence.

Miriam was one of our earliest girls, and she led us every kind of a dance. In her low state of existence she claimed all our help and patience. Her rudeness and crudeness were fascinating. She could be defiant and filthy. She brought out all our reserves and often left us bare of ideas. There was often nothing more we could do. Church House was just a convenience for her. She had had a poor past, so that the comfortable bed we offered, the bath, the clothes, the food, were almost too much for her. In a careless, coarse way she was attractive, and her violence and scorn of us matched this.

Nora was especially close to her, and Miriam would call her "Mum". This made it all the more difficult to deal with her. She was with us a long time. There was a special boy friend, and I was a bit dubious, but he was given access to the house. It ended when I walked into the lounge one evening to find them, in the company of two other girls, Miriam and her boy friend full length on the settee, locked in each other's arms with a rug over them.

Still we stuck to Miriam, but she used to go out from Church House, wearing red skin-tight trousers and a jumper, into the most notorious Maltese café. Her candid descriptions of what happened in there were like a personal confession. I had to send her from Church House to the gutter. She went to rock bottom with heart-break, drugs and fits, and was picked up and taken to a London hospital. It was there that the staff and patients tried to make out what the semi-conscious, raving girl was crying for. " 'Sneel, 'Sneel, 'Sneel," she went on, until by luck a girl from our area interpreted it as "Miss Neal". Very soon after Nora got to the hospital I was there myself. The Mum-touch had calmed her, though she was still in a bad way. My presence revived her more, but not in the same way—she gave me more than the length of her tongue, and blamed me for everything; for I had turned her away from Church House.

In spite of this, her deep affection for us all has held. We have to make the best of a bad job. She is now well out of the area. She is not living to our liking, but it is a thousand times better than it was. For a long time now, she has been living with a man who loves her and works for her. She has a husband elsewhere, but I think there will be a divorce, and with it stability will come to her present relationship.

More tragic is the story of Clare. We had a call from a certain hospital, telling us of a patient who was being pestered by the man who had been living on her. She had tried to get away from him, but he had traced her to the hospital and was threatening her. All through visiting hours, he would sit by her bed, and he kept the hospital under constant watch. We arranged to kidnap her. On the appointed day, I took my car to a side entrance and the ward sister, who was the only one in the secret, got her dressed and out to the car, and we whisked her off to our second house, where nobody knew her story. She seemed to be settling down well, and was very happy. Then something unforseen happened. A girl we had known for some time was bashed up by a thug, and was afraid to go on living alone. We took her in. By bad luck, Clare was known to her. A day or two later they had a quarrel which ended in fighting, and I had to ask the other girl to leave. It was only the next day that Clare went out to her job in an A.B.C. and did not reach there. From that day to this we have never heard of her. We can only assume that she was forced to go back to her "protector", but although we knew all her old haunts, and informed the police, we have never seen her. It is easy enough for girls such as Clare, with no relatives and no roots, to be put out of the way, and nobody would miss them.

Some girls we only meet for a brief space of time, but cannot easily forget. It was in the summer of 1959, when Church House had not been going very long, that Liz was sent by a probation officer. She was on probation from a South Wales town, and had come up to London to get some glamour. She was an attractive girl. Nora got her a job at a local factory. In the evenings, Liz used to go out, saying she was going to see her probation officer, but after she had stayed out all night once or twice, Church House decided they couldn't have her playing ducks and drakes with them. I gave her a good talking to, and so did Nora. Nora wrote to her parents, saying we were sending her home, and meanwhile a bed was booked for her at a reception centre.

As it happened, Audrey knew nothing of these arrangements. So when the vicarage door bell rang at 11 p.m., and there was Liz, Audrey asked her in. Liz explained that she was going home on holiday the next day, and Church House was full up, and what was she to do? Audrey put her up in our spare room—I had already gone to bed, and she told me nothing about it.

Next morning, before I went out to the church at 7 o'clock, she told me Liz was there. I told Nora, and learned that the police had been looking for her all night. The probation officer phoned to tell Audrey that she had Liz's ticket, that a W.V.S. car would be along later to take her to Paddington, and that on no account were we to let her go off alone. At breakfast, she dissolved into tears, and said she would not go home; then, after something to eat, she cheered up, and went upstairs to get ready. Then she said she must go out to buy a pair of stockings, so Audrey found her a pair. A few minutes later she discovered she had no lipstick, and she could not go without any make-up. Luckily Audrey found some spare lipstick and make-up and we at last managed to get her into the car without letting her slip through our fingers.

One of our particular friends was Kate, who had had polio as a child, and had a bad shortening of one leg. She had been earning some sort of a living as a prostitute's maid, and she came to us in a filthy condition, tired out, with her leg iron broken, which had caused ulceration of the leg. She was sent to the London Hospital for treatment, and gradually improved physically. She was an excitable girl and full of fun. One night she had been playing ping-pong in the club room downstairs, and came rushing up into the kitchen and slipped and crashed on to the floor on her bad leg. At first we were afraid she had fractured it, so I got an ambulance to take her to the hospital, where she had already spent hours that afternoon. Fortunately, it was only bruised. Kate stayed with us for some time, and now she has a job in the west country where she is doing well and is very happy.

Our work is for prostitutes and girls in moral danger. Many of the girls who come to us are certainly not hardened prostitutes, but I feel that my insistence that the word "prostitute" should be included in the constitution of our Wellclose Square Fund was justified, for in the absence of a clearly defined purpose there is a danger that the Fund and our houses might be used in the course of time to deal with women who have never been tempted to prostitution. My fellow-workers have sometimes objected to the use of the term, for several of the girls we take in have drifted into prostitution through other weaknesses. Some are alcoholics, some are drug addicts, some are only weak in mind. Yet we know that the odd pound or night's lodging they get for sleeping with a man is very useful to them. What they all have in common is that nobody, except the men who use them, has any time for them. We are there to give them what help we can.

We have many friends in our work, not least those religious communities who support us with their prayers and generous gifts. Then there are the voluntary helpers who come to us in the evenings, at week-ends or for longer periods, to do anything that needs to be done. What a lot I could say about these grand women, with some delightful youngsters, hospital nurses among them, who have gathered round me to care and slave for their sisters who are in need of real love. They are among the great souls, for they do not place themselves above those they help. They know that but for the grace of God they might have been where their friends are. They put up with insults, even violent attacks from some of them, without flinching. They will scrub and clean, they will take their friends to V.D. clinics and sit there with them, knowing what will be thought by all and sundry. I want to make it clear that the work I started could never have been properly begun, without these good and gracious women.

After the house had been opened for about two years, I wrote a letter of encouragement to all our staff and helpers. By this time we had got over the experimental stage. We had arrived, and all sorts of knowledgeable authorities were interested. Over a hundred women and girls had shared the simple home life of our bright and cheery house. We had made mistakes and learned some lessons. We were a family.

I told them I felt that this family atmosphere was itself a very obvious sign that God was with us. Without consciously "being

L

like Jesus" or trying to live out the salvation we preached, they were doing just that. Hard work, easy work, or just sitting at a meal, we were happy being together.

That this happy atmosphere has influenced the girls there is no doubt from the many letters we have received: "You will never know how much you have done for me. You have made me feel that there is something worth fighting for." "If it wasn't for you and the ladies at Church House I just wouldn't have anyone to care whether I lived or died." "Every morning and night I say my prayers and I never forget to ask God to bless you in the great work you are doing. Keep on praying for me, Father, as I need all the prayers and help I can get . . . Please write back soon as I shall be counting the days till I get a letter from you." "I promise you that I shall do my best to repay in every way this wonderful chance that I have been so lucky to get—and as long as it is in my power, I shall not let you down—but please, please, do not ever give up hope for me—just hold on to me so very tight, and never let me go."

It would be useless to pretend that many of the girls who leave us "go straight". Of 250 who have stayed with us to date over half have kept in touch with us. Some, like Rhoda, have gone back to their families. Others are in prison or mental hospitals. Some have been back to us again and again. In answer to those who criticise us I would say that we have never claimed that we will reform them all. What is important is that none of them can ever say again, "I was never given a chance." I believe quite simply that this is the Lord's work we are doing, and if we ever feel like condemning these women we would do well to remember that it is that same Lord who said to the Pharisees: "Many who are street women will go into the Kingdom of God before you."

CHAPTER V

The Beginnings of Public Support

THE summer of 1960 was an important time for those of us who wanted to see drastic changes in the west end of Stepney.

1st June was a red-letter day, for Lord Stonham, with Lady Ravensdale, was following on the failure of a Private Member's Bill in the House of Commons to deal with the licensing of clubs and calling for magistrates' power and control of clubs.

Some weeks before, Lord Stonham had asked me if he might use the statement on certain clubs which I had sent to the London County Council. I suggested that he might come and see for himself. He was shocked at our conditions as I took him round. We went into half a dozen cafés and met the people. At the end of his visit he said, "I shall have to rewrite the whole of my speech." I told him I felt that would be a very good thing, for he would be writing from knowledge and not just from hearsay and report.

A small band of us went to the House of Lords and sat through nearly four hours of speeches and debate. We watched bishops come in and we watched them go out until only one remained. I thought this a particular scandal, for I had written personally to the Archbishop and other bishops, and anyhow they must have known the kind of things that were going on. I felt sad. My voice in Stepney seemed practically a lone one. But I had written to everyone I could think of, from the Prime Minister down to the Local Authorities; from the Commissioner of Police down to the Superintendent of Police in Leman Street, from the Archbishop down to the Rural Dean. To all these I had made known the conditions of our part of Stepney over the past years. Now this scandal was to be burst open by Lord Stonham and Lady Ravensdale. The seriousness with which Lord Stonham took the matter up made me write to him and say that I was sure that the clubs would be curbed and the rottenest parts of Stepney cleaned up now that he had started the ball rolling, and it would be one of the best things he had ever done in his career.

The counter-blast to Lord Stonham's effort and the very full press it secured came from the Rural Dean of Stepney, Prebendary Young. There can be no question as to the Prebendary's general support for my cause, and his recognition of the downward drift of Stepney. But he wrote to *The Times*, minimising the infected area and stressing that the greater part of the Borough was all right. This was followed by a longer letter from the Leader of the Stepney Borough Council, Mr. Jim Olley, emphasising the same thing and adding that Stepney could not be recognised "by the reports put out." These letters forced me to raise the issue in my July "Pilot", which was sent to every authority in the area, to M.P.s and the rest. I headed it, "A Plea to the Minister of Housing, the L.C.C., the Mayor and Borough Authorities, religious leaders and the people of Stepney." In the bravest print I called upon them to "condemn and destroy all the hovels and slums now, and give Stepney a real chance!" As against the two letters to *The Times*, I pointed out that no less than four parishes were infected in the worst possible way: St. Paul's, Dock Street, St. George's-in-the-East, Christ Church, Spitalfields, and a fourth parish, almost as bad in a different way, the parish of St. Augustine's and St. Philip. These areas have grown in evil as decent people have been driven out. They cover a good mile in length from East Smithfield through Dock Street, on through Leman Street, over the main road, through Commercial Street to Spitalfields Market and spread a similar distance to the east. In the middle of this is Toynbee Hall where the Chairman of the Stepney Fabian Society lives. Mr. Moonman, like the Rural Dean and Mr. Olley, chose to minimise the shocking state of the area. He wrote a letter to the *Guardian* in which among other things he said, "There were a few old women, methylated spirit drinkers, some years ago in Stepney, but there are none now." Mr. Moonman is an important man and his words carry a lot of weight. I could not get my letter, in reply to his, in the *Guardian* but I wrote to him, and informed him of the uphill task of the Rev. George Appleton, at St. Botolph's, in trying to do something for meth drinkers. I have my full share of them in my parish. Mr. Moonman is but a few yards from St. Botolph's Church and not so far from mine, yet he just didn't know.

I was sure that it was quite wrong to play down the shocking conditions regarding both prostitution and housing in Stepney. The Government and Opposition, the London County Council, the Local Authorities and the Churches must be forced to recognise the horrible truth and to do something about it.

That issue of "Pilot" also included pictures of our hideous slums, taken by my churchwarden, Frank Rust. Before the war there was much talk of these foul buildings being demolished. Bombing had made them dangerous, but all bombing had been over for seventeen years, yet the derelict buildings still stood, like horrible ghosts gloating over the vice (with the juke box accompaniment) which they witnessed.

The "Pilot" brought Sir Percy Rugg, the Leader of the Opposition in the L.C.C., to Stepney. I took him round and showed him Church House. We also went to the notorious Sander Street, subject of one of the pictures in the "Pilot". Those of us who had watched the worsening of this festering sore, had been told over and over again that the buildings, which were the property of the L.C.C., were empty and clear of prostitution. But although the roofs of the filthy dwellings had been demolished, the soliciting went on in all weathers in the lower rooms. By then (1960) the law had been passed to stop soliciting, and the Police Superintendent of Thames Police Court stated at our August meeting that any offences would be dealt with. When I took Sir Percy Rugg to that street it was worse than I had ever known it. The girls were at the windows with their arms on pillows or cushions and we were solicited although I was wearing my cassock and biretta. These Sander Street hovels could be seen from Commercial Road and men were always looking from the main road. In the half-light the girls' faces looked like the pictures you see of witches—thin and haggard and dirty—and their voices matched their work and conditions. When we reached the end of the street, Sir Percy said with horror, "And I am the landlord of that!"

The houses came down a few months later. I was at home in the vicarage one day when Frank Rust rang me up and said, "You must see this, Father, they're pulling down Sander Street." Of course I lost no time in hurrying round to see the glad sight, and when I saw all those filthy hovels coming down, I just fell on my knees there in the street and said a *Gloria*. I did not know that Frank had taken a photograph of me until I saw it in the *Daily Mail*, and of course all sorts of things were said about it. People accused me of specially posing for the picture, of trying to make a sensation. But the only thing that was in my mind at that moment was a great surge of thankfulness to God that this foul place was at last being done away with. Yet even after the crazy houses were demolished, the more stable house on the corner of Backchurch Lane was used as a brothel and soliciting point; the landlords were prosecuted and had to pay a heavy fine.

I did not let up for a second agitating about the hovels and prostitution, and I did not hesitate to use the gentlemen of the Press when they telephoned or came to see me. I had hopes and promises and excuses from the authorities whom I pestered. To keep the ball rolling, I felt the Diocese might do more and I wrote to the Bishop of London asking him if he would kindly consider allowing me to address the London Diocesan Conference about our conditions in Stepney. He replied that he would like me to do so. It was arranged that I should address the Conference on 13th February 1961. It was further agreed that Edith Ramsay should follow me. No one better could have been suggested, for she has worked in Stepney for over forty years, and Stepney people have a great affection for her.

The resolution before the meeting was: "That this Conference considers that derelict and slum properties in the Diocese, and particularly in the East End, encourage prostitution, and that the sale for profit of such property, and the raising of rents unaccompanied by improvements, is a social evil. The Conference requests the Minister of Housing and Local Government to ensure that Slum

Clearance is pressed forward vigorously; particularly in the East End of London."

Edith Ramsay and I spoke at length, and gave as clear and downright a picture of conditions as we could, ending with an appeal to Church and State authorities to do all they could to do away with this scandal. The Resolution was carried unanimously, and was sent with a covering letter from the Conference to the Minister of Housing and Local Government.

We felt that at last we might be getting somewhere. The next day we had an excellent press, and the *London Churchman*, the official publication of the Diocese of London, gave the whole of its April issue to our cause, with telling pictures of our Stepney area. I contributed an article, telling something of our work, and the Bishops of London and Stepney both gave our work their full support.

One thing leads to another.

The morning after the Diocesan Conference, I had a good post, but the letter which gave me the greatest joy was a simple word of praise from the Dean of St. Paul's. He said he was deeply moved. With his letter he enclosed a five pound note, not for the work but for me. I felt the thrill of sixty years before when I had had a penny given to me; it was an occasion. But in my thanks to the Dean I had to remind him that a few years before I had written asking him to allow me to preach in the Cathedral. This time he did not hesitate to offer me the only vacant date for 1961, nor did I hesitate to accept the twenty minutes offered on Sunday, 23rd July.

But much was to happen before that. It did me good to go to St. Thomas's Hospital and talk to the nurses the evening after I spoke at the Diocesan Conference. I had a very full Lent, and except for the help of Nora Neal and Daphne Jones on Sunday mornings, I did everything and loved doing it. Time was found too for several talks outside about our special work. The most important was the Christian Team Work lunch talk. It was a very full meeting; all sorts of business men were there with at least two M.P.s. I pinned up lots of pictures of our Stepney slums and derelict buildings. I pulled no punches about the slums, cafés and clubs and their responsibility for the most glaring evils of the district. One M.P. had been trying hard to get fellow members of both parties who were working on the Licensing Laws to come down to Stepney, have lunch at the Red Ensign Club and see the area. Everything was arranged and then it was cancelled, and nobody came. How much legislation is passed into law without knowledge at ground level? Certainly, much oratorical hot air goes up without an idea of the true facts.

The Bermondsey Social Group did me good when I spoke to them. I shall never forget the incredible shock and the silent horror when I repeated the words of a "classy", upstage prostitute I saw in my study, who quite casually referred to the boys of one of our most famous schools coming to her.

Lent 1961, Holy Week, a grand procession of witness at Deanery strength on Good Friday evening, after the morning services and the Three Hours' Devotions, gave me the strong and settled assurance of my faith as a Christian. Easter was as good as it can be in Stepney. During Lent I had talked to six parishes in and out of London, all about our special work at Church House. During the three weeks after Easter I was to give another six talks. The new responsibility felt by the Church through the launching of the Christian Stewardship campaign has made quite a difference to us, for seven parishes are now giving us help regularly in money and service.

Nora Neal and Daphne Jones both have a share in speaking out of the parish and are in great demand. Those two ladies had gone in turn for a rest after Easter. I planned to go away for two Sundays, and stayed away for many. After three days at Wittering I was in hospital with a painful attack of glaucoma in my one seeing eye.

Since that awful Monday, 24th April, when Dr. Lee of Wittering had me taken to Southsea Eye Hospital by ambulance, my friends have been concerned about my future. At that particular time my mind was not so much on my own future as on the future of Church House and the burden on Nora Neal in particular. I think her singleness of purpose surpasses my own in wanting to help to the utmost girls who have fallen into prostitution or who are in moral danger. The work would continue while Nora lived. Only a few minutes together were necessary, at our first meeting nearly five years before, to assure me that here was the woman who would never turn back to lesser duties. With age she may give place to a younger woman, but she will always in all humility and with the wisdom of God alone give this work, and those engaged in it, her loyalty and love.

So I lay and pondered as engagements had to be cancelled. I assured my Bishop that if I felt unequal to my tasks I would not hesitate to give up my parish and give what strength I had left to my special work. He sent a kind letter saying, "I see I have got you down to preach at St. Paul's Cathedral on 23rd July. I hope you will be really well by then." I did not tell him, but I was determined to go into that pulpit and say what was in my mind even if I had no sight.

The relief from pain in my eye was heaven itself. I had misunderstood the specialist, for I had thought that treatment might rule out the need for an operation. Anyhow, when he told me that without an operation I should lose my sight, I asked him to operate. He felt it would be more convenient for me to go to Moorfields Eye Hospital. I saw Mr. Perkins at Moorfields and he performed the operation. A few days afterwards, he assured me that I should have no more trouble, though my sight would be less.

On the Sunday following the operation, I made my Communion. The Chaplain hadn't come to the ward, and it seemed a little strange when the nurse called out on Saturday night, asking who wanted Communion. The day before I went out, I was able to take a young blind man to the chapel, where three of us were present at Communion.

A general ward is a good place for a priest to be. To be one with men and youngsters and to come under a common rule is good for us, and we should be examples to the others. Because I expected and accepted no special treatment, and because I put the lovely flowers sent to me in a place for all to enjoy, I was fully accepted.

At first the men who were admitted with me hated the thought of a parson being in the ward. One man who found that not only was he to share a ward with a parson, but was to live beside him in the next bed, did not hide his disgust. I took it, but I was determined to break his prejudice down. The opportunity came when we both learned that we were to be operated on soon. We both wanted to write home and tell our wives. It was like me to forget writing paper and stamps, but how glad I was to have forgotten. I called across to my neighbour, "Lend us a bit of your paper, chum, so I can write to me missis." His eyes said, "Blimey, he's human." He came straight round from his bed and gave me paper, envelope and stamp. It wasn't long before we were comparing notes and he told me all his feelings about parsons and exactly what he had thought about me. We had our operations; we saw to each other's needs; we talked about the things that mattered in life, our people, our friends; we said good night religiously when one or the other tired; we were friends.

I had been most anxious not to miss my son's ordination to the priesthood on Sunday, 25th June. Mr. Perkins took care of that, for I was out in a week.

It was a joy to be with Tony, Barbara and Ruth, their lovely baby. Tony had to go into retreat and so Audrey and I were company for Barbara. My thoughts were on the future of this little family. My mother used to say, "While I have a pair of hands we shall not starve." Those were brave words sixty years ago, for there was no work to match the will to do it. But here was Tony refusing ordination in the normal way. He went into a factory instead of into Holy Orders when he had finished at the Theological College. The authorities didn't like it and there was a minor struggle between Tony, who knew that he was meant to be a priest, but a priest doing the normal man's job, and the Bishop of Oxford and his advisers pressing for the usual procedure, full time in a parish. The Bishop finally decided to ordain Tony after he had been in the factory for two years, and to attach him to a parish without pay and allow him to go on with his manual labour at Pressed Steel, Cowley. It seemed utterly stupid to me to keep Tony waiting for ordination because of the work he was doing. He was not asking to be let off examinations, and few would dare to say that he lacked the spiritual vocational power. The advantage of more hours at his books and perhaps on his knees, could never make up for the experience of taking off his coat and doing eight hours a day side by side with ordinary work-men. Tony must tell his own story one day, but it gave me very great joy to see him priested and to be at his first Mass and to be communicated by him.

The day following, I went to my proper convalescence. As it is difficult to get any peace or complete rest in Dock Street, the almoner at Moorfields arranged for me to go to the Old Rectory, Elstead, and by the great kindness of the Matron, Mrs. Cook, who made me rest, I had a most glorious fortnight just before my date at St. Paul's. At that lovely house I finished my sermon. A kind lady who has a most lovely cottage at Elstead, typed it out for me, and I tried hard to pay her for her long and difficult task, but she won, bless her.

CHAPTER VI

Sermon in St. Paul's

THE Dean of St. Paul's had made a point of telling me that I could only be allowed twenty minutes because Sung Eucharist was to follow. I read over my stuff and could only add and add to make it clearer and I knew I could not compress it into the limited time. Yet I knew I was meant to say every word. Then, to complicate matters even more, Frank Rust appeared on my doorstep on the Saturday evening, the day before the date. "You must come and see the Parkers, Vicar, there are twelve of them sleeping in two small rooms." I wasn't a bit keen and it was a drag to Royal Jubilee Buildings, and although they were in my parish nine years ago they are not now. I could not have been less enthusiastic, but when Frank, Stepney born and bred, says you must see a thing, then you must. I was not sorry when I arrived there. On my way I recalled another family who lived on the top floor and had no roof, but a weighted tarpaulin as a shelter. I saw the Parkers and their terrible conditions. Frank and I returned to the vicarage. He told me to put the family in my sermon, but the thought of meeting the Dean after my sermon was preached concerned me very much indeed.

My own church people wanted to hear me in the Cathedral, so I arranged the services so that they could be there, and I could cover my own work. It was a very hard day for me. Arriving at the Cathedral in very good time, the Virger met me with a healthy smile and said, "I am glad you are preaching, Father." I thanked him and told him to take me by the hand and tell me what to do, and he did it all beautifully. The last thing I wanted was to talk nothings, so I went to the Lady Chapel and knelt there until six minutes before 10.30. I went to the vestry and met Canon Collins, then the very kindly Prebendary Paulden, an old friend who looked all the blessings he wished me, then the Archdeacon of London. Then the miracle happened. The Dean arrived, shook me warmly by the hand and said, "*Say all you want to say and don't hurry.*" I literally sobbed inwardly with gratitude and relief.

I loved sitting next to the old Dean, the lovely voices of the boys and men enchanted me and my mind went back to the time when it was thought I might be a Cathedral chorister. I remembered, too, how I knew I could never make the grade nor be accepted, for I was boss-eyed, ignorant and desperately poor. There has never been a day when I have missed thanking God for all His goodness to me. I have felt it so much and been so thankful and happy and honoured about it that I wonder when the great big bump will come to try my faith truly. I was perfectly contented to be there in that lovely Cathedral and become passive to it all.

I was quite calm as I made ready and awaited the Preachers' Virger to conduct me into the pulpit with dignity. The result of my three months' pondering was in my hand scored in a rough way for emphasis. When I had settled in my own mind what I had to say, I had sent a copy to Tony and Barbara, and asked them to comment if they wished, but I did not consult any other person. It was worked out without fuss and on a basis of prayer. There was no pique or grudge meant, it was the truth.

The script of the sermon as it was preached
in St. Paul's Cathedral on Sunday 23rd
July 1961

"In the name of the Father and of the Son and of the Holy Ghost, Amen.

"Yesterday was St. Mary Magdalene's Day. Over six years ago another Mary cursed me in the street for passing her because she was a prostitute. I reassured her. Later Mary came to me with a simple present, which I tried to refuse and, quite properly, I received another cursing. I accepted the present and then knew that I had received a commission from God to do all I could for women and girls in that terrible business.

"Nearly three years ago my two women colleagues set up Church House, Wellclose Square, not half an hour's walk from here. They made it their home and into that home they have received over 150 women and girls and made friends with many more. Now we have a second house ten miles away from Stepney. Your prayers and your money are needed for this work.

"All who have lived that kind of life, and those who are still in it, are out of the normal stream of experience. *If they were normal in the beginning, then turning night into day, taking pep pills, drinking too much and often taking to drugs; these things, added to their immoral and sadistic work, cut them off from ordinary people.* Further, it brings to them the feeling of being outcast. In their misery and bitterness, they flaunt criticism and, of course, justify condemnation by cursing, fighting, cruelty and general viciousness. There are, too, mentally weak girls and our Welfare State does nothing about them unless they go raving mad or of their own accord go into a mental hospital. I am *quite* sure that if a girl cannot look after herself and has no one to care for her, she should be cared for under restriction. Our effort is to make a way of escape from prostitution for those who are still reasonable and have a little to think with.

"We think often that in our freedom we are superior to Russians. A little time ago a Russian newspaper said our slums of Stepney were a disgrace. Again a Russian V.I.P. stated here, that there was class distinction even in the cleanliness of areas, the City and good residential places are spotless, other areas filthy. *I doubt very much if the Soviet Union would allow half-wits and mentally weak girls to be enslaved in prostitution as we do. Further, I am quite sure that the Soviet Union would not allow the lazy and the louts of their men to live on the immoral earnings of women.* Among those men convicted of that crime here are many who are in receipt of Public Assistance. Here is one, recorded in the *East End News* of 23rd June; the man had done no work for two years and had received £5 7s. 0d. a week from the National Assistance Board.

"It was Hitler who said the British were a decadent nation. It wasn't true, *but where are we now*? Often our national attitude is hypocritical, the faults and needs of other peoples are condemned by State and Church and other oddments of Societies, and the horrors we live with at home are overlooked or ignored. We who try to make Stepney a better place are called all sorts of things for speaking the *truth*. Only the other day a man of some standing tried to get me to say that Beverley Nichols' article on our part of Stepney was exaggerated when in fact it doesn't cover half the horrors. Again, the new Chairman of the Stepney Fabian Society wrote to the *Guardian, with the tone of authority and under the address of Toynbee Hall*, saying, among other things that there were now no methylated spirit drinkers in Stepney. The *Guardian* did not publish my reply, so I wrote to Mr. Moonman and asked him to allow me to address the staff of Toynbee Hall about conditions in Stepney and told him of the excellent work of George Appleton, the Rector of St. Botolph's, Aldgate, for down-and-outs, and particularly for meth drinkers. In reply to my letter Mr. Moonman declared himself on my side in wishing to clean up Stepney, but thought that no good could come from publicising the bad conditions. That is the attitude of Government, L.C.C. and Local Authorities—put your head in the sand and do nothing.

"It is fitting here to thank the Press, Radio and Television for their great help. The angle from which I condemn apathy and neglect is above *politics*, above *party*, and as a *Christian* and a *Parish Priest*. From that position I shall continue to pester all responsible authorities until, not twenty-five acres as is promised, but the whole of the Stepney slums, including the horrible tenement buildings, are condemned and destroyed and the people rehoused. Last evening my churchwarden, Mr. Rust, told me I must go to the Royal Jubilee Buildings, Wapping. We went to a flat where we found Mr. and Mrs. Parker who have been there for thirteen years, and their ten children, living in the most terrible conditions I have yet seen in East London. The living-room is about 12 by 9 feet, the other two about the same, where twelve of them sleep. On Wednesday next we are told that the Housing Minister is visiting the slums of Stepney, *but only if he has time* will he go to Royal Jubilee Buildings. From here *I ask him to find time*, and take with him Mr. Leader of the L.C.C. and see that flat if he isn't sick before he gets there, and I ask him not to miss the W.C. The landlord isn't known to the tenants and the most cruel racket is being practised in that mass slum, for youngsters who want to be married put down £22 and try to put into repair the most horrible, bug-ridden rooms. Press take note. May I be allowed to plead with the Chancellor here, in his impending restrictions on spending. Whatever spending you cut down, sir, let it not be on new houses or on the clearing away of slums and bombing relics.

"But I want to address myself to the churches and in particular to our archbishops, bishops, dignitaries, as well as the ordinary clergy and people. I hope they won't mind if I turn their eyes to the people and conditions needing their attention most. Often I feel that our Church of England, and other Churches for that matter, are top heavy with intellect and words irrelevant to present conditions, and not understood in the slightest by the people. Added to that, real Christian deeds are lacking. Not forgetting my own weaknesses and sins, I feel we have lost sight of our real business, to warn, change and save people. Our churches, vicarages, palaces often save us, protect us, from being the shepherds we are meant to be. Like Amaziah to Amos the prophet I might well be told to go and earn my bread elsewhere, but like Amos I think we are like a basket of rotten fruit. Often the kind of lives we live prevent us from seeking sheep that are really lost; keep us from being really interested in the fight for better things. I think often it is easier for the people to pray for Angola, South Africa, and the Congo, and even give to the poor wretched refugees, *which indeed must be done and done more*. It is easier for Church authorities to do and urge these things than to clean up our own country and people.

"When Lord Stonham and Lady Ravensdale spoke in the House of Lords of evil clubs and our terrible conditions in Stepney, I dared to hope that the Archbishop would be there and would take part. He said he would if he could, but he didn't. On that great day there were three bishops in the Lords, and when the Bishop of Chester was introduced there were six. At that moment I was made to think of the "ten little nigger boys", for all but one bishop went out before the debate. The Bishop of Carlisle was the one bishop left. Although it was Stepney's two individuals who initiated the gallant work of Lord Stonham and Lady Ravensdale, the Bishop from the north had to be satisfied with what Miss Ramsay and I wrote to him about Stepney. I only mention that to illustrate that the top Churchmen knew about the horrors of evil clubs which were springing up in their hundreds and are still with us. If we judge from what archbishops and bishops have said *consistently* and *publicly*, what they know and think of *evil clubs, prostitution* and the *ever growing industry of evil men living on the immoral earnings of our girls, it is nothing.* The Bishops of London and Stepney are the exception, but they will be the first to admit that their interest came alive through the work of the small band of pilgrims in Stepney. The bulk of our clergy feel like a bishop, who wanted to come and see our work and conditions in Stepney. He said to me, rather weakly, 'How shall I dress?' How shall I dress! as if perhaps he were in another country.

"I am not saying these things because I am bitter or have a chip on my shoulder. I say them because the Church and churches have slipped into a wet and weak attitude and are in danger of losing sight of their vocation. Literally our hands are too clean, and we are too damned respectable. As things are, can we imagine an archbishop or bishop finding time to live for one week in a year, in the toughest parish of his diocese, without a shield around him? For the most part our leaders know very little of the practical side of winning souls and being one with the people in their difficulties. Most of us are inclined to 'lord it' and become *Mass* priests and *leaders* to a small band of the faithful. *Is it not true that many of us feel it is no use, and a waste of time to seek and to save those who would seem to be lost? Yet* that is what we are called to do. The Church authorities are set too far away from the scenes of hell and degradation; too far from the life which drags down and claims so great a number of our young people. Note how the B.M.A. last Monday tells of the alarming increase of venereal disease among young people, and I wonder if the Church authorities have ever known so many doctors talk of the help the clergy might give in this field? *We must all* endure the insults, the cursings, and the spittings which come from being at hand to try to help. The pictures of the Master we need most in this highly organised and mechanical age are of His humility and humanity. The Lord who was God took a bowl and washed

M

the disciples' dirty feet. He didn't pretend to do it. It took a long time to wash twenty-four feet. How many of us would do that? I experienced this kind of humility over thirty years ago when my chief, a dean of a cathedral who had had the best in birth and education said, 'Joseph, will you please hear my confession?' He knew I was born in the slums of London and had neither his fortunate breeding nor his education.

"A brief turn to the Master's humanity. The ecclesiastical authorities of His day were tied up with their dignity and authority and missed their true calling of caring for or even considering the poor, the sinner, the lost. No contrast could be greater than the attitude of heart and mind between Our Lord and the Pharisee as the prostitute anointed and washed Jesus' feet. The Pharisee poured silent scorn on Jesus and judged Him as not being a prophet because He allowed the woman to touch Him. Jesus condemned the Pharisee and forgave the woman her sins.

"Listen to the tears in these words from the hearts of two prostitutes to me. There could be many others. 'Father,' (one says) 'I shall always thank God for His mercy in leading me to you. I do hope you won't mind me writing this, but I really feel that if only there could be somewhere like Church House in every big city and town in the country, it would be a big help. I only wish there had been somewhere like it years ago and I am sure I wouldn't be sitting where I am now.' *That was written from prison* where I and my two women colleagues in this work, Nora Neal and Daphne Jones, have visited her regularly.

"Listen to this from another:

" 'Never in all my life, have I received such kindness as I have done from you and the good people of Church House. I shall never let you down. But please, please, do not ever give up hope for me. Just hold on to me and never let me go. I shall never, never go back to my old way of life and living.'

"Our work at Church House and our other house, *is less than a drop in a bucket* compared with the need and what the Churches should be doing in Britain.

"It is a long time since Mr. Reeves, the most kind honorary secretary and treasurer of the Wellclose Square Fund said, 'Most of our donations come from women.' Without women this work could not be done at all. She won't like me saying it here, but Miss Nora Neal has borne a greater weight than anybody in this work and, I think, shed more tears, and secondly, Miss Daphne Jones, in a different way has been pure treasure over three years. They have suffered me with their burdens. One other has done her share and suffered me very much longer: my best investment, my wife.

"*Great excitement was caused* when the last Archbishop saw Pope John. I want to pay a tribute to The Legion of Mary, that Roman Catholic voluntary band of humble women, who, *with our own most excellent band of voluntary workers and of other denominations, forget differences*, and our denominations, when the soul of a girl is to be saved by loving kindness. *Stupid men say we mustn't pray with words together*. Many times during the past three years the collective silent prayer offered, has been met by the angels and taken to the throne of mercy in the shape of a prostitute saved from degradation and hell. Good deeds are much more important than good words; to work is to pray.

"Will the Church and churches heed the words of Mary the prostitute who handed me my commission? She says, 'I really feel that if there could only be somewhere like Church House in every big city or town in the country it would be a great help.' The Church Commissioners, the Church Assembly, the Diocesan Conferences should have this need before them. But although we must have a very great deal of money, a far greater difficulty is to draw truly dedicated women and priests to this work; for the venture will fail unless true homes like Church House are established.

"I conclude with an appeal from this Cathedral pulpit to all people of good will to back a material, practical, and most Christian action *I am taking now*. Almost without exception, the 153 women and girls who have come to us have said, 'I never had a chance.' We accept that, but we reply at once, 'You can never with real truth say that again. Here is your chance.'

"I know that many hundreds of our British girls are living in slavery, under men who are living on their immoral earnings. They are living in this country of ours, often under threat of razor and gun. I call on these girls to come out of it and go to the nearest police

station and claim protection. Shelter must be offered to them by
the churches. Up and down the country we have thousands of
friends of Church House. We have also Moral Welfare branches in
every diocese. Open your houses and your hearts to these girls. I
call upon the archbishops and bishops to back this Church work
with vocal support and material help.

"Christians must not allow any girl to be enslaved by an evil man
in this way for lack of a shelter and a way of escape.

"Practical help in this way is the Lord's own work and is priceless,
and so very close to the Saviour's heart, who was so kind and good
to women."

After the service in St. Paul's I walked out with the Dean, who
had kindly asked me to lunch, and the then Archdeacon of London.

Sadly, the Archdeacon was displeased with me and said so. A
much higher dignitary than he said almost the same thing: "We are
all behind you in your good work, but you have spoilt it by attacking the bishops." This kind of talk infuriates me, as did the editor of
the *Church Times* when he said something similar. The fact is, the
bulk of Christendom is too far behind the front line and most
bishops are the "Brass Hats" of old. They are behind me in condemning the Government, the L.C.C., the local authorities; they
are behind me in fighting vice and setting up places of escape for
prostitutes; they are behind me when I am suffering persecution;
they are behind me as I go on alone until my head spins and my feet
won't carry me and I fall exhausted on my bed. They are behind
me and yet can't find me a priest to help me. Yes, the truth is the
the authorities are too far behind.

As we walked out of the cathedral, the Press and photographers
were in full cry. The Archdeacon wanted to know who all these
people were, and I wondered if he thought they were my personal
friends. It was so hot that I had to tell them I would give a Press
conference at 3 p.m. that afternoon in my vicarage. At lunch with
the Dean there were three of us, the third a charming young lady, a
German student. I enjoyed my lunch, but enjoyed the Dean more,
the ease with which he spoke and the natural sparkle in his eye. We
had a deal in common, not least a love for the Cathedral, and I told

him how I had climbed over the ropes when the Cathedral stood, surrounded by burning buildings and falling walls, at the end of 1940. He knew all the men who meant a lot to me. But I think I enjoyed most his general talk about the deans before him and who should have been what. I owe the Dean a very great deal for allowing me to preach in his Cathedral.

When I reached my vicarage, I had time for a short rest before Frank Rust had the drawing-room full of reporters and photographers. My good wife kept the tea pots full. It was of course my first experience of a Press conference and I was kept busy with questions. They didn't spare me and I did not hold my punches. We roared with laughter over and over again and we forgot all about time. When they did go, I felt very tired, but I knew that whatever they got into their papers, I personally could not have been more honest nor candid with them.

What a press I had on that Monday! The Church and its work marked a lengthy report and photograph in *The Times*, and the *Daily Sketch* very nearly filled its paper with comment and quotations. I was not eager to broadcast on the B.B.C. and I did not do it very well.

On the Wednesday, 26th July, the Minister of Housing came to Stepney and I met him at Royal Jubilee Buildings where the Parker family live. We were all televised. In the evening Sir Donald Kaberry, M.P. and Mr. Norman Pannell, M.P. came and saw Church House and the area. While we were having coffee the telephone bell rang and my wife called me as it was a personal call from Paris. The operator then put me through to a Dutch doctor who said he and a lady who was with him were very interested in my work and wanted to help. "We are going to give you a very large sum of money and I want you to tell me how I should make it out." I said it was very, very kind of them. I then spelt out the name of the honorary treasurer of our Wellclose Square Fund and his address. The gentleman then asked some details about our work and asked me what money we had in hand and he went on, "It is a very large sum of money we are giving you, it is *seventy-two thousand pounds*"; he repeated it. I kept my head and I was deeply moved and thanked him again. His was the cultured, unpretentious natural voice of the perfect wealthy gentleman of perhaps seventy years of age, and I believed him absolutely. When he spelt out his name, I said, "and your address, sir," but he would not give it over the telephone. I went into my drawing-room and told the two Members of Parliament and my wife and expressed my grateful wonder. I might easily have blazed the news to the world but my visitors counselled quiet patience. How wise they were, for I have heard nothing since from my generous friends in Paris. But God has been very kind to me. He has given me a steadiness that even the promise and non-fulfilment of £72,000 will not shake.

In this same busy week, the Bishop of St. Albans asked to come and see me on Thursday evening. It was to be a private visit, but very soon after the arrangement was made, the daily press were on to it. Somebody had let the cat out of the bag, Stepney was becoming a zoo and it just wasn't good enough. Moreover, I still meant to live in it. The Bishop was surprised when I told him. We altered the day and he came on Friday afternoon. Nobody could have been more gracious. He saw all we had to show him. To put him, Nora Neal and Daphne Jones at ease and away from my possible domination, I left the three of them alone. We had tea in Church House and after tea, I took him to the Franciscans in Cable Street. Father Neville received us. We went to their chapel and although it was, of course, Father Neville's position to ask the Bishop for a prayer and blessing, I found myself asking for both. Father Neville has been my confessor since I came to Stepney, so he will find room to forgive this added encroachment. St. Peter has nothing on me in speaking first. Anyhow, it was a priceless few minutes we spent on our knees.

The Bishop and I walked the length of Cable Street and passed the time of day with everybody and looked in the doors of a few cafés. After seeing the Bishop off, I got in a very short rest before I was on my way to Cardiff to televise with the Bishop of Taunton at 10.30 p.m. It was nice to see him, but I felt it was ridiculous to have him there to answer my criticism of bishops. Here was a bishop who had worked in East London as a parish priest for twenty years or more, and that I think is almost unique.

The Bishop and I got on very well. He made his point about the need of brains and I stressed the need of brawn, brains and common sense. I said I was sure that the Church should aim at reclaiming more men of the people for priests among their own. Scholarship never added up to true ability without practical experience. Our twelve minutes ended with my saying some straight things about prostitutes. Coming back to London on Saturday morning, I knew I shouldn't have gone. I had been too tired to sleep and was exhausted. I lost myself for a few minutes in the empty carriage and put my feet on the seat and so got a tongue-banging from the train-guard. He was quite right and I all wrong. When I reached home I found I had left my very nice nylon pyjamas behind and had lost them. What a life!

Although only two bishops took me to task for saying the things I did in St. Paul's Cathedral, others wrote to me in most gracious terms. One diocesan said, "Personally I accept your rebuke (and that of others) that we bishops are too far removed from the coal face." Another wrote: "There is indeed something terribly wrong with the Church as it is today, and the remoteness of its bishops from the sinful and weak is only a symptom of something far bigger ... Thank you for your courage, and may God give you His strength and every blessing."

CHAPTER VII

The Work Goes On

THE Wellclose Square Fund's growth is a token, a showpiece of what can be done. Indeed, a Probation Officer in the North of England said, after reading *Father Joe* and its sequel *Friends of Father Joe*, "We could do with one of Father Joe's houses in every one of our big cities'.

It is twelve years since my sermon in St Paul's Cathedral—which followed the addresses made to the London Diocesan Conference by Edith Ramsay and myself. I dealt with the horrors of prostitution of teenagers from Ireland, Scotland, Wales and from Northern and Midland towns (very few were Londoners). Miss Ramsay dealt with slums and housing. In the area of St Paul's Dock Street, Stepney, demolition and building has gone ahead and the prostitution has shifted but not diminished.

Wellclose has three houses now: in Stepney, Goodmayes, and in Birmingham, and over two thousand young prostitutes and girls in moral danger have been given homely care and love by our Wardens and their staffs. In addition, girls come to the houses for advice, and sometimes simply to talk. I have told some of their stories in *Friends of Father Joe*.

Since I felt the definite call from God to make a way of escape for prostitutes who want to get out of that life, the work has become my life, all of it. The aim is two-fold. I know that I am meant to press Christians to be really outward looking. To see and to feel what is happening under their noses. Let me illustrate. I have just been to Birmingham to see a Chief Inspector of Police, an appointment made after a protest by me to the Home Office, then to the Public Prosecutor's Office, and finally, to my Member of Parliament. There had come into my hands a most vicious and filthy magazine with the printer's name printed boldly on it, and, more boldly, the address and name of its editor. Inside was a list of a hundred prostitutes for hire.

Being in the area, I went to our Wellclose House and sat down to dinner in the kitchen with ten others, staff and girls. It was a full house and a happy one. After dinner I talked to Bridget, a student who had come to the house to help in any way possible until she went to college. I listened while she told me how her parents had been anxious about her coming to Wellclose House. They had come with her, and before they had met anybody her father had said, "This is a homely place, you will be all right here." She told me what the house had meant to her. It had opened her eyes to a deeper relevance of her church services and of her life to the needs of girls who could be helped. She preached to me from my own platform, on my own subject and with the elation it gives me. Sadly, so many people "don't want to know", and could not, without awkwardness, take a cup of tea with youngsters who were "lost and have been found". There might be some excuse if the need were growing less, but the opposite is the case. In 1961, "one hundred and thirty men were sent to prison in London alone, for living on the immoral earnings of girls." In 1971, the number was two hundred and two. The true picture is very much worse, for few men are arrested as we are terribly short of police.

In the very early days of the venture, a Sunday newspaper gave the Fund £200 for three articles by me. We only had one house then. My first effort was headed on the front page: "To all prostitutes. You need not go on in that life any longer; here is a way of escape." It worked then for one girl. Now our work is well-known and our houses are stretched to the limit. We lack staff and the staff lack sleep and proper time off.

So I come back to my heading: our work grows and "is but a token, a showpiece of what can be done". How can I blaze, as I want to, from the housetops, through the press, to every young prostitute: "Here is a way of escape; there is nothing we will not do to help you out of that life"! I can't do it, because we are bankrupt of the kind of women's help we must have. Life-giving it must be, for the staff must be available night and day. Women of the sort we need are with us now, but far too thin on the ground. The work is led by Angela Butler, who served the toughest apprenticeship in Stepney and became Warden of Church House, Wellclose Square. Seeing the worst parts of Birmingham, she was drawn to it. I visited her before there was a Wellclose House and shared her problems. We saw young people together, and sat in cafés together. She worked alone, having nothing to offer young people but her friendship.

By her witness and her love, Angela Butler was known when Wellclose House, Trafalgar Rd. was opened by a member of the Cadbury family, and blessed by the Bishop of Birmingham. She won Jean Hodges for the Stepney work and there could be no one better. Sister Paskin of the Church Army has charge of the Goodmayes House, with the help of an old friend and former Warden, Sister West. In Birmingham, Angela Butler has been joined by Sister Mary Catherine SSF and by Miss Williams, a Methodist SRN. From time to time Sisters come from Roman Catholic orders to help in and learn about the work. In my most recent book *In Honour Bound*, I pay tribute to the work done by our women workers and appeal to other Christian women to come forward and give some time to help in the rescue work. It would seem that it is only to women that I am speaking. Far from it, for we are going to fail in this work if bishops and priests, pastors and ministers are frightened of the subject and are afraid to ask women to consider this work for their sisters?

Look at it in the light of our existence, our Church existence. On the whole we are good at keeping our churches going. Are we not far less good at doing the Church's work, its real work? Can I hear bishops and clergy say, "he shoots a line"? Please wait a second! After my notorious sermon in St Paul's Cathedral, an Archbishop, now dead, wrote to me. He rebuked me and said, "You want me to do your job as well as my own. . . . ? I am sure I was right when I replied, "I could not do your job for a minute of time, but I should always expect you to do mine because you are a priest as well as an Archbishop." Much nearer the mark came a Diocesan Bishop's letter which said, "There is indeed something terribly wrong with the Church as it is today, and the remoteness of its bishops from the sinful and the weak."

It is in the parishes and in the parish churches that we see the strength or the weakness of our Christian mission, and it is from the lips of the clergy that the laity will be moved to consider special work and service for God. We can be so much braver and stronger if we only let God in. The 1971/72 *Crockford's Clerical Directory* is prefaced as usual by some distinguished anonymous churchman. It is full of the truths of our declining moral standards. "Standards of sexual behaviour which have been accepted since New Testament times are now openly called in question by some of the clergy, not only in books but on the radio and television. Millions of viewers are given the impression that the Church has now abandoned its moral standards." It is good stuff, for he castigates the BBC, the newspapers, and our bishops too. He says, "The Church is paying a heavy penalty for the past inadequacy of the teaching of moral theology in the universities and theological colleges." I think somehow that "moral theology" would put this anonymous, most able writer on the spot for hiding his identity. What a stinging difference it would make if it were written with a name to it, for so much of what he writes needs to be said. It is tough going to follow the Master all the time. To stand up and be counted as Christians is not easy. We become sensitive, and involvement makes heavy demands upon us; yet we are no good at all unless we are absolutely involved. We *are* committed, and there is no turning back when we allow ourselves, unreservedly, to share a real burden. I am committed to the care and protection of young girls.

Prevention is always better than cure. That is why I try to get into the schools. Within a few months I have been to five big schools for girls of various sorts. I tell the girls about my own background and the rescue work; I tell them about prostitution among young girls, of VD and the 300,000 new cases in 1971 (50,000 more than in 1970). I tell them that their virtue is their greatest treasure.

I was invited to one school for three days and so was able to develop a closer working relationship than just me talking. Question time brought: "Do you think that girls of sixteen should have the pill?" To some, sex was all that love meant. I found general, common-sense reasoning was the best approach. It is my view that girls generally get the worst of it in sex relationships. "To love and leave" is more common in boys than in girls. It is very difficult to exercise any kind of self-discipline after the sex act has begun. It means excitement, pleasure, and it also can mean disappointment and depression. For both the young and the mature it is difficult to get on with normal work and activity. A very young and intelligent couple I know, fell physically in love, got married, but after just a few months, were sad and bored. It can be much worse for the young girl who has given herself, outside marriage, and been left. It can undermine her self-respect and be the first step downhill.

It is possible for young people to win through, but discipline is not popular. As Sir Frederick Catherwood has so ably said, when speaking of the self-seeking, all for "number one" attitude rife in present-day society: "Girl friends are disposable. Unborn children are disposable. Wives and husbands are disposable if they have become ugly or irritating, or if they have failed to flatter their partner's vanity. Children are disposable. Old people are disposable—packed off to a Home as soon as they become a nuisance." He goes on to say: "Some people call this a civilised society, others call it a permissive society, I call it an irresponsible society."

Much of that may be true, but it need not be. The great majority of girls and boys, young women and young men are open and honest and basically good people. Last year, Bishop John Robinson recommended that the age of consent should be lowered to fourteen. Recently, the learned barrister. Mr Gordon Scott, said he feels strongly that the age of consent should be fifteen. Both would protect boys in law. Mr Scott says, in the *New Law Journal* of February 22nd, 1973: "Unfortunately in many cases today in which teen-age boys are concerned, it is they rather than the girls who are in need of protection." That may well be true; but I feel strongly too. I see very clearly the danger to young girls, coming not so much from teen-age boys as from grown men. I know, and so does Mr Scott, that judges are not fools and would deal with a teen-age boy as a boy. A girl will naturally be attracted to boys of her own age or a little older, but young girls, especially the emotionally insecure, frequently find older men attractive and are flattered if they receive attention. An attractive and unscruplous man can easily seduce a young girl. A fourteen or fifteen year old school-girl may, as Bishop Robinson says, be "mature" physically and "ready" for sexual activity, but emotionally and mentally she is still a child. This is an everyday situation, but Mr Scott, as a barrister, will remember a shocking case which came up before Mr Justice Forbes, of young girls exploited and kept virtual prisoners in a vice ring. He will know that I do not exaggerate.

It is significant that the pressure to lower the age of consent comes from men. Fathers of girls of fourteen, fifteen or even sixteen may feel very differently, especially if their daughter becomes involved with a man and leaves home. Because she is of the age of consent she cannot be brought back home before it is too late. When infatuation has worn off, or the man has wearied of her, her case is pitiable.

Because our rescue work among young prostitutes is at the very grass roots of the problem, we are anxious to meet and fight every attempt to lower the age of consent. I am cheered, at the time of writing, by the reassurance of the Minister of State at the Home Office, Mr Mark Carlisle, who says: "The Government has no plans for amending the law to reduce the minimum age of consent to sexual intercourse." The Minister informs me that the age of consent was raised from thirteen to sixteen by the Criminal Law Amendment Act, 1888. He refers me to the Latey Report of 1967, and the recommendation that the age of consent should remain at sixteen.

When it was still very far from the end of the war, Sir Winston Churchill spoke of "the end of the beginning". That could be the case with our rescue work. . . "the end of the beginning". I have pleaded many times for a million pounds, and indeed I do now. The truth is that given the right people, the rest would follow; we

should not want. All my friends will remember that there was a
beginning to this work, when I hadn't a penny, and my income at
St Paul's, Dock Street was £500 a year. I was called to do it when
I hadn't a Woman Worker, and when I was glad of the small rent
coming from two families in Church House, Wellclose Square.
God does things. The work has lived from day to day and, in the
sight of the world, it has lived perilously close to the end. Faith
and devotion by a few have carried it, and in the battlefield of the
work it has been women who have carried on the fight. These few
have endured the strain and stress, even violence, not without
some casualties, and, because they care, their burden is all the
time increased by their own efforts.

The work is a constant reminder to the conscience of this
country, and its churches, of the degradation of prostitution. I am
reminded of Joan, a delightful young girl, still well under twenty.
She had just finished her first experience of Holloway Prison. She
wanted her clothes and was afraid to go alone to try to collect them.
So off we went to Islington in my little car. She said little during
the journey, afraid of the man we might meet, who had been
something more to her than the landlord in return for her one room.
He was in and said he knew nothing of Joan's cases. I told him
I should have no hesitation in going to the police for help. We got
her things. Joan's relief was obvious. She was now free and relaxed
and smiling. She told me bluntly that prostitution would have
driven her mad if she hadn't taken a full day off a week. She went on
to tell me what she did on her day off. She dressed simply, and
generally went to a public dance hall where she was quite unknown.
She would pick up a poorish lad of her own age, treat him to a meal
and take him to a good film. They danced and had a drink. I
listened and waited for the sequel. To my surprise she said: "I
took him to a spot near my place and kissed him goodnight."
With all the solemnity possible she assured me that only by
behaving normally for a full day a week did she keep sane. I
believed her absolutely, and the awful picture she drew of her work
as a prostitute confirmed it. She hated herself for the life she had
led and the clients who had used her. Most of them were family
men, and all of them were glad to leave her as quickly as possible

after the contract was completed. It was always depressing and cold. This picture of Joan is just nothing beside the existence and cruelty suffered by so many in this life.

Even now I have the word "exaggeration" flung at me by people, and I am told "there will always be prostitution." Will there? Just as we are meant to remember and help those who starve and suffer in under-developed countries, just as we have to care for the old and homeless, the drug additcts, the alcoholics and the unwanted, we also have to remember and help the thousands of young prostitutes who can be kept outside our vision by prejudice, hypocrisy or humbug.

The year of this new edition is marked by our Rally and Service of Rededication of the Wellclose Square Fund. As Founder, I felt that something of this kind should take place, to give all our friends an opportunity to meet; to thank God for all his love and blessings; for the work done over the years from my Stepney days, for the staffs in our three houses and for all our voluntary workers, for all our friends known or unknown, and for the blessing of never being in debt. To thank God for our Council, and especially for Robin Waldron, our Honorary Treasurer and Secretary, who was also our very first Auditor, for our Committees and for all who help in any way.

In this same year, the BBC, for the seventh time, gives our Fund the "Week's Good Cause". It is to all England, and our President, Bishop Trevor Huddleston of Stepney makes the appeal.

"First things first" heads the dedication of this book. I was helped in many ways in writing it, but not in its dedication. I began with God and I end with God. Without him the story could not have been told, nor could it have happened at all.

Born into poverty, I was crippled with TB, my sight was poor and I had a bad squint. So ignorant was I that I could only with great difficulty scrawl my name—at fourteen. I was laughed at because of it. A good singing voice was my only gift, and it landed me in the church choir. My good mother went to work when she was still a child. She never went to school and could neither read nor write. Not a good start for a boy who was to be a priest! There were those I looked up to, but the only educational help I was to receive before I was twenty-four was from my dearest and most generous friend, Father Noel Lambert.

I often wonder when I am going to wake up and find it is all a dream. I could not believe my good luck when I found myself in St Saviour's choir. I found the God of love then in the midst of dreadful poverty and starvation. I learnt to pray, and heaven was worship in the midst of horror. In that setting I felt the call to the ministry and it never left me. Nor was I free from temptation and sin; nor am I now. What has become a part of me is a continued, in-built sensitivity to sin in thought and deed, so that I feel, as a matter of course, I must get back to God. This to me is a matter of fact and habit. Sin never lays me out in depression and helplessness or doubt. I just know all the time that my Redeemer lives. I find myself saying: "Lord, take me up and do not let me down". That negative is with me when I have failed and when I know I just cannot conquer without him. It's a cry for help.

So I come to my attitude to prayer. I am a relaxed person, and as a relaxed person I can be heatedly provocative and condemning. This has not always been the case and I have suffered for it. I am able, under God, and now as a habit, to let many things affecting me pass over without a gesture. Because of this passivity I am able to cope. I begin with God: Father, Son and Holy Spirit. Whatever the material or personal urgency, I begin with God. The problem is then cut down to size. The pressures in Stepney would have killed me if I hadn't given them to God to sort out. I went to God and gave them to God. He told me how to cope. From my knees I could get up as a giant. My approach to a problem is the same as my approach in prayer. My hands are always open. My whole self is handed over. My "Stepney" line of approach was in my two little prayers from the heart:

"Lord, be a lantern to my feet, a light to my path,
Show me the way to go."
"Please God, teach me to love your company more and
more."

Being in the company of God, and being in the company of man for God is to know that the Incarnation did not begin and end at Christmas. It is in you and me, day by day, for mankind.

If you would like to contribute to the work described in Father Joe,
donations should be sent to :
M^r̶ ~~The~~ Rev. Joseph Williamson,

40 SUMMERFIELD ROAD
WEST WITTERING
CHICHESTER
WEST SUSSEX
PO20 8LY